Moving Beyond
The Christian Myth

Moving Beyond
The Christian Myth

The Next Step in
Our Spiritual Evolution

by
John W. Sloat
Former Presbyterian Minister

CCB Publishing
British Columbia, Canada

Moving Beyond the Christian Myth:
The Next Step in Our Spiritual Evolution

Copyright ©2011 by John W. Sloat
ISBN-13   978-1-926918-94-5
First Edition

Library and Archives Canada Cataloguing in Publication
Sloat, John W., 1932-
Moving beyond the Christian myth : the next step in our spiritual evolution /
written by John W. Sloat – 1st ed.
Includes bibliographical references.
ISBN 978-1-926918-94-5
1. Christianity--Controversial literature. 2. Religion--Controversial literature.
3. Bible--Criticism, interpretation, etc. 4. Spirituality. I. Title.
BL2775.3.S56 2011   230   C2011-907072-3

Publisher: CCB Publishing
               British Columbia, Canada
               www.ccbpublishing.com

<u>Dedication</u>

To our three children

Linda Ruth Sloat Burig
Laurie Ann Sloat Silverstein
David John Sloat

who have struggled with me
through my conversion to
Heresy

and who have been unfailing
in their love and support.

I am very grateful.

Contents

Introduction

If you read my previous book, *A Handbook For Heretics,*[*] you know something of my story. I was a Presbyterian minister for forty years. In 1980 I had a sudden spontaneous past-death recall. Up until that time, I had been a doctrinaire conservative who fit into the old time belief system of the church. But that event completely changed everything. It turned me from a mainline Christian into a new thought spiritualist who was fascinated by all the mystical experiences being written about these days. I launched a website which invited people to share their spiritual stories, and eventually collected hundreds of them from all over the world. But that resulted in getting me kicked out of the ministry, primarily because I included reincarnation among the various topics on the site.

A Handbook For Heretics was written in the hope that the church would broaden its outlook to include information about Near-Death and Out-of-Body Experiences, as well as other mystical events, including the recollection of past lives. But the longer I reflected on the Christian tradition from my forty years as a pastor, the more it became clear to me that it was time for a major overhaul in our thinking about religion, God, and true spirituality.

What follows in these chapters is my spiritual worldview. It may not be yours. This will not be a scholarly work, so I will not burden the text with too many footnotes or references. I will make certain claims without much documentary support because it is not my purpose to prove anything. I want to sketch out a vision of what is wrong with the old system and where I think we should be moving in the coming century. I believe that all of these assertions will stand up to scrutiny if you care to do the research, as I did in preparation for writing this book. If my vision triggers sympathetic vibrations in your own soul, I am glad. That means we have something to discuss.

If it does not, I would urge you to think about what I have written before you write it off. After you do so, you are perfectly free to throw the book into the fire and dismiss me as a heretical lunatic. You will not be the first one to do so.

I believe that the world is ready for a new spiritual paradigm. In fact, I think the corner has already been turned. The generations now coming into the world are less religious and more spiritual than those which went before. This is progress. Jesus said in John 16:12, *"I have much more to tell you,"* and promised that when the Holy Spirit comes, it will lead us into all the truth. The Holy Spirit *has* come, and I believe that God is revealing this additional information to us every day. The question is: Are we listening?

How does God convey that information to us? In the same way as always, through the mouths and writings of prophets. I can only hope that the Spirit will allow me to be one of the minor prophets, and will use my personal vision to inspire the minds of others who are seeking a larger truth.

All cultures, as they mature, move from myths developed in the past to clearer and clearer visions of the truth. God is Truth, a truth so profound that we can only glimpse tiny fragments of divine reality. And so we have invented myths about the spirit world to fill in the gaps. Then we make those myths into divine revelations and end up worshipping the very stories that we ourselves have created. It's time to end this process. Perhaps we will accomplish nothing more than creating new and more sophisticated myths. But we must at least cast off the myths of the past and attempt to update our vision of the spirit world.

We begin by reexamining the myth that Christianity is the only approved route to heaven. And we conclude that it is not. But if we dispel that myth, what do we put in its place? What will our view of the spiritual world look like in the future when we have dispensed with the ancient stories about God that we inherited from our forebears? That is the answer this book will attempt to provide.

I must add a technical note here. Anyone writing about God these days wrestles with the use of pronouns. Do we use the old form, referring to God as "he," or do we use "God" in place of every pronoun? "God gave us God's revelation so that God could reveal God's will to us because God loves us as if we were God's only child." The only appropriate reaction to a sentence like that would be "huh?" Such an attempt at political correctness would interrupt the narrative flow as abruptly as a block of concrete thrown in front of your car. God is not a man. Or a woman, for that matter. (He) is both and much more. So, for the sake of style, and to prevent unnecessary headaches for both of us, I am taking the easy way out and using "he." I will, however, make one concession: I will capitalize "He." Since I don't use that form for human beings, it will make it clear about Whom I am speaking. And you will remember that He is just as feminine as He is masculine. Thank you.

I am going to begin most chapters with a rather bold statement. The statement for Chapter 1 is: *Christianity is a religious myth.* Some people have said that this sounds like a conclusion, and that I should state it in the form of a question: *Is Christianity a religious myth?* I have thought about this carefully, and have decided to go with the former approach. I want to state my conclusion at the beginning of the chapter, and then try to demonstrate why I believe the statement is true. I hope that this method will help you think along with me.

My use of the terms "church," "religion" and "Christianity" are, for the most part, interchangeable. But there are slight differences. The term "church" refers to the whole Christian Church. "Religion" is a reference to the general category of religious activity. And "Christianity" of course is a specific reference to that religion. The context will, hopefully, clarify any confusion.

All the stories of mystical experiences that follow are original, and have been contributed to our website by their authors from all over the world. We would be happy to have you visit our site where you will find many other stories. You might even have an experience of your own which you may be willing to share.

I want to thank three special friends: Sally Dexter, an accomplished graphic artist, for the effective illustrations in Chapter six; Lynn Morgan, who designed the cover of the book and put up with my endless tweaking of her original ideas; and Tom Huston, for his faithful support and encouragement. I am very grateful to all three of them.

All scripture quotations in this publication are from the Good News Translation in Today's English Version-Second Edition Copyright © 1992 by American Bible Society. Used by Permission.

Feel free to contact me at the addresses below to share your stories or to react to the ideas expressed in this book.

J.W.S.
September 2011

Check out our website at: **www.beyondreligion.com**
or write to me at: **john@beyondreligion.com**. Thank you.

*CCB Publishing, British Columbia, Canada, 2009
Available on Amazon and Kindle

<u>*MYTH*</u>

* A story of ostensibly historical events that serves to unfold part of the world view of a people or explain a practice, belief or natural phenomenon.

* A popular belief or tradition that has grown up around something or someone; especially: one embodying the ideals and institutions of a society.

* A person or thing having only an imaginary or unverifiable existence.

Merriam-Webster Dictionary

Prologue

How Religions Begin

I once found a toad in the stairwell leading down to our cellar door. Surrounded by the corpses of many of his fellows, he was frantically trying to escape his concrete prison before he became one more casualty. I caught him, carried him up the stairs and put him on the lawn. As I left, I wondered how he was going to explain this experience to his friends that night.

"Listen to what happened to me," he might have said, bursting with awe and excitement. "I fell down a great cliff into a terrible hard, dry place. Others of our kind had also fallen into this pit, and their bodies lay all about me. There was no way to escape, and I was certain that I would end up like the others, dry and lifeless.

"Then a miracle happened. An enormous hand reached down from heaven toward me. I was terrified because I thought this was the Being who killed toads. I tried to escape its grasp, but it kept relentlessly pursuing me. When it finally caught me, I was sure I would never see any of you again. But, before I knew what was happening, I found myself on the cool earth among the grasses. And then the great hand simply went away.

"There must be a god who saves lost toads!"

His story might well have become the main topic of conversation in the toad community. They had certainly never before heard of a toad god, and might have wondered what to do about this revelation. Perhaps, a few days later, the toad took them out to the edge of the cliff over which he had fallen, and let them peer down into the frightening depths where he had been trapped. Then he might have taken them to the spot where he had been carried to safety by a power greater than himself. They could well have marveled at this miracle, realizing that it had forever raised their level of awareness. Imagine the scene:

One of the older toads says thoughtfully, "I think we should come out here every week to recall what happened to our friend. We should stand at the cliff and remember how he fell, and then come to this spot to remind ourselves how he was raised to new life. And I think we should meditate for a moment on the fact that there is a god who saves lost toads."

Pointing to the rescued toad, he continues, "You could tell your story over again, and then we could all say something together in toad chorus, something like: 'The [god] reached down from above and took hold of me. He rescued me. He helped me out of danger.'* And we must be sure to tell our toadlings that there is a god who saves lost toads."

After a while, some of the wiser toads begin to wonder why their friend had been saved when so many of their brothers had been left to perish. And it occurs to them that this toad must have done something to please the toad god, while the others might have offended him. And so they draw up a long list of rules which they think might please their new-found deity. They want to be certain that, if they ever fall into a dark pit, the great hand in the sky would be inclined to reach down and save them, too.

In later years, while everyone knew the rules, the original toads died off and no one was left who remembered actually talking to the toad to whom the miracle had happened. The story was passed down from mouth to mouth for many years, and the more superstitious toads in every generation faithfully followed all the rules. But in time, the details of the story were lost, and it became nothing more than a myth which parent toads told their toadlets at bedtime.

*Psalm 18:16,17,19

Chapter One

A New Age

Christianity is a religious myth.

I was a Christian minister for over forty years. I preached all the traditional doctrines, told all the old stories, assured my congregation that the miracles were all true, and agreed that Christianity was the only way to get to heaven. Now I am convinced that I was wrong. I was trying to sell them an ancient myth disguised as God's truth. How could I have been so misled? And how do I deal with the memory that, for all those years, I was misleading my people?

What follows is my attempt to atone for all the ways in which I went along with the factual distortion that calls itself religion. To correct that distortion, we need to be able to say: *The Christian religion is a mythological attempt to explain the unexplainable nature and plan of God.* If the church can make this statement, and admit that the things it is saying are not *literally* true, then this faith tradition can continue for uncounted centuries into the future, as a beautiful metaphor which helps us live in the presence of God. If it does not make this statement and come to terms with its mythological origin, if it continues to insist that what it teaches is literal truth, more and more 21st century people are going to realize that Christianity's message is medieval superstition, and I fear that the church will gradually be abandoned as irrelevant.

Following is a story which does not fit the belief system of traditional Christianity. We need to think seriously about how a congregation should respond to one of its members who tells this kind of story.

A Phobia Cured
I have always had a horrific fear of spiders. Any kind of spider. Once, I saw one on the ceiling of my bedroom and spent the night in the living room. Another time, I woke up a room-mate to kill one that was in the bathroom. And I was an adult when these things happened.

Many years ago, a friend of mine asked me to go with her to a lecture by a woman named Denise Linn. She was talking about reincarnation and was going to do a "group regression." Being a skeptic, I agreed to go just to support her, but I was laughing in my mind.

I have no memory of what triggered this, but suddenly, during the regression, in my mind's eye I was a small boy in the desert. There was a man on a camel looking down at me sternly. I was his son. Suddenly, a big black spider crawled up my leg and bit me, and I died.

When I came to, everyone sitting around me was asking if I was okay. Apparently, I had been screaming. I laughed it off.

Six months later, I noticed that there was a spider in my kitchen. I casually scooped it up, put it in a container, and took it outside. Then I suddenly realized I had been doing this for many months. I stopped dead in my tracks and thought, "Wait, I am terrified of these things."

The change was dramatic. I have no explanation, though I do think about that experience with the regression. Could something have been resolved?

None of the ideas expressed in this story are part of the Christian worldview – regression, reincarnation, psychic healing. Does that mean that they are not real and that the author is simply imagining these things? If they *are* real, are they ideas which threaten the Christian teaching, or should the church investigate them to see whether they might be part of God's truth?

The search for spiritual knowledge has always had two levels of awareness, myth and truth; that is, religion and reality. Religion is what we think we know; reality is what we can never fully know, at least on this side of eternity.

Religion, with its history and traditions, speculates about what heaven is like. These speculations include all sorts of images – sitting on a cloud playing a harp, walking down streets paved with gold, enjoying the company of seventy virgins, living in gorgeous mansions, experiencing endless bliss. It all depends on which religious culture you come from. But most traditions agree that we will spend eternity in that other world doing...nothing. Religion is curiously unclear about what will occupy our time once we get to that other world. Perhaps that's because there *is* no "time" on the other side.

Opposing those religious speculations is the reality of the spiritual world. About this we know little or nothing. So in our quest for information about the other side, we are caught between guess-work on the one hand and ignorance on the other. Not a very solid basis on which to draw meaningful conclusions. Yet, guesswork and ignorance have always been the building materials from which religion has constructed its theology.

However, a revolution, a huge paradigm shift in our spiritual thinking, has been taking place in the last thirty-five years. It began in 1975 with the publication of Raymond Moody's groundbreaking book, *Life After Life.* Moody provides evidence that human beings can exist outside their bodies, in spirit form. Religion has always taught that we will live in spirit form in heaven when we die. That belief is central in the belief systems of religious people, but it had previously been an unproven article of faith.

Yet, here came scientists – scientists, mind you, not religious professionals – reporting that the church's ancient teaching was true, that people *are* able to live apart from their physical body, and not just after death. Four years prior to Moody's book, Robert Monroe had published his own investigations in a book entitled *Journeys Out of the Body,* a record of his personal Out-of-Body Experiences (OBE's). Eventually, he established an institute in Virginia in which he taught people how to go out-of-body. Here were clinical data from two sources indicating that we are in fact dual beings,

3

incarnated spirits, that those two states of being are separate, and that we can experience existence as spiritual entities, under certain conditions, *here on earth*. This was a watershed moment, a triumph for the religious establishment: its belief that the soul is a reality separate from the body was now confirmed by reputable science.

So, the world of spiritual understanding changed forever around the third quarter of the 20th century. For two millennia we had had nothing but myth and tradition with which to map out the contours of the other world. But now we moved into a new age in which we began to assemble a vast library of revelations about the domain of spirit, filled with all sorts of testimony from people who have been given insights into its reality and nature. The authors of these modern scriptures were just as inspired as those who wrote the books of the Bible, and they need to be taken just as seriously.

All of this new information seemed to support Jesus' statement in John 16:12, that he has much more to teach us, and that we will learn this new truth when we open ourselves to the voice of the Holy Spirit.

These modern revelations are helping us understand that spiritual reality is far different than what we were taught in Sunday School. What we are learning is that entrance into the spirit world is as simple and natural as crossing the line between the United States and Canada. Easier, in fact, because we don't need a passport stating what religious culture we come from. Religion has nothing to do with crossing that border. Entrance doesn't even depend upon our being "good"! That world is our natural home, and we all go back there when we die, sinner and saint alike.

The spiritual world is all around us, on a different vibration level, and it is as open and free as a meadow in spring. However, when religion approaches that meadow, the first thing it does is erect a fence around it, build a gate and start charging admission. But the church doesn't own that field, and so it has no right to take possession of it in order to deny entrance to others. Christianity claims that God gave the church the right to lock certain people out.[1] But we know that this is nonsense, since the field belongs to everyone whom God has created. Even the thief on the cross went to heaven immediately.[2]

The Christian Church is in the business of trying to understand and teach the nature of the spirit world. It does that by a combination of revelation, superstition, guesswork and intuition. And that is adequate for any given moment in time. But human knowledge and sophistication change over time, and inadequate views of the eternal need to keep pace with those changes.

An inscription in the Jefferson Memorial in Washington, D.C. quotes a comment by Jefferson in a letter he wrote in 1816:

> I am not an advocate for frequent changes in laws and constitutions. But laws and institutions must go hand in hand with the progress of the human mind. As that becomes more developed, more enlightened, as new discoveries are made, new truths discovered and manners and opinions change, with the change of circumstances, institutions must advance also to keep pace with the times. We might as well require a man to wear still the coat which fitted him when a boy as civilized society to remain ever under the regimen of their barbarous ancestors.

The problem is that Christianity has *not* rushed to embrace these new revelations, as you might expect it would. Rather, what it teaches today is essentially what it taught 2,000 years ago. Yet, that old theological package is not large enough to contain the new ideas. There are many things we know today about the interaction between the spirit and physical worlds which are not in the Bible. Many of us want to add these things to our religious belief system because we believe that they will keep the church from dying of irrelevance.

The church has resisted these new views for a variety of reasons. Religion claims the spiritual world as its exclusive province, maintaining that science is competent to make authoritative statements only in the realm of the physical. So, it asks, what right do these scientific people have to meddle in questions about the nature and activity of the soul? Second, the idea that we are free to leave our bodies at any time is a total rejection of the church's claim

5

that this separation can take place only after death, and only on the authority of God. Third, the kneejerk reaction of large portions of the church has been that this information must come from Satan and is designed to distort and destroy the church's ancient teaching.

So, western religion, rejecting Jesus' promise to tell us much more, continues to turn its back on the Jesus whom it claims to serve. The church is so wedded to its ancient myth that it has turned that myth into an idol which it worships, ignoring and even attacking these new revelations. It's no wonder that younger generations, who are far more open to these new ideas, are being described as more spiritual and less religious than their forebears. They are the ones who can see the exciting possibilities suggested by stories like the one above, possibilities which promise a whole new understanding of God and His plan for all of us.

It is fear that is holding back the advent of a new spiritual age. People are afraid that the new ideas might be wrong, or even demonic, and so they hold on to the old myths just to be safe. But those views have caused innumerable wars in the name of God, and have created endless divisions in the human race, divisions which this new truth has the power to heal. If people understood the real nature of the spirit world, and our connectedness within it, it could trigger a new era in our spiritual evolution, one which could revolutionize the planet and unite us all as one family of God's children.

Thus, we have a choice between listening to tradition – looking backward – or being open to the Holy Spirit and looking forward to a new age. It's a simple matter of ancient myth vs. current revelation. If the church insists upon focusing on the former, many of us will have to band together and embrace the latter.

Chapter Two

The New Myth

I am saying that the Christian religion, as it is now practiced in most places, is a myth. It began with a man who lived in Palestine 2,000 years ago, a person with a powerful message and a magnetic personality, who was killed because the authorities saw him as a threat to their power. His followers, devastated by his death and reflecting on his teachings, spun his life into a new religion. They borrowed miraculous stories from other religions to inflate his image, and eventually came to believe that he was God in human form. The religion they invented, which has been passed down for eighty generations, is primarily legend, misunderstanding and guesswork concerning God's plan for humanity. And it has remained essentially unchanged for all that time.

Recently, as we noted in the previous chapter, we have moved into a new age of revelation. We have been given insights into the spiritual world which are significantly different than the view outlined in scripture. I referred to this fact in the first chapter without indicating what those differences might be. I want to do that now, so that we will have a basis for comparing the new ideas with the old as we think about what constitutes a myth.

I have called the present religious worldview a myth, and indicated that at a number of points it is wrong, in light of the new material we are receiving. We cannot know the whole truth until we eventually find ourselves on the other side. So, while each new set of revelations gets us one step closer to the ultimate truth, we cannot expect to understand that truth thoroughly while we are still in the flesh. In an attempt to be ruthlessly honest, therefore, I am calling this updated vision of the spirit world "the new myth," so as to avoid suggesting that it is the full and final truth. I am convinced that it is much closer to the truth than current religious doctrine is, but to avoid being guilty of the same kind of hubris with which I fault the church, I feel compelled to admit that every step toward the light leaves us with a new and larger mythological image, perhaps truer than the old, perhaps not.

Our view of the spiritual dimension of our life must necessarily begin with our ideas about God. What is God, what is His nature, what was His purpose in creating us, and how does He judge the quality of our life when it is over?

These questions are at the very heart of religion, and most of them are unanswerable. Which is why religion has, for the most part, invented the answers. We have good reason to believe that God is loving and benevolent. But we know that He is not some sort of exalted human figure – or any kind of figure for that matter – sitting on some kind of heavenly throne. He is more of a creative energy force than an individual being, yet He has the ability to relate to us – call it a personality – which is why we call Him "He" instead of "It." But we can't let that pronoun mislead us. We realize, when we look at the universe, that some unimaginably powerful intelligence has put it into motion. How did God get started in the creation business, and what significance does a physical world have for a spiritual deity?

Moving on from these mind-numbing questions, we realize that there is nothing but God. Before He created the Big Bang there was nothing, unless the Big Bang itself resulted from the implosion of a former universe, a kind of reverse Big Bang, what we might call the Big Sucking Sound. In that case, we can think of the universe as God breathing in and out, expanding and contracting, each exhalation creating a new set of realities. What does He create these realities from? Well, God doesn't have a warehouse in which He stores planets and microbes and all other life forms, including us. As the Bible bears witness, when God creates He simply says, "Let there be…" and there is. And the thing that is, is created from the life force that is God. So we are part of Him.

The Bible is correct again, therefore, when it says that we are made in His image. It would have been even clearer if the record had said we are made of His essence, His substance, His own nature. And the fact that we all come from the same source means that we are all part of one another. Physically we have different blood types, but spiritually we all have the same soul type, regardless of sex, race or religion. This idea could have a profound impact on the human race if we would come to terms with it. What we do to others we do to ourselves.[3] We *are* that other person, and we need to study the implications of that fact. "The self and the other are just two sides of the same coin. To understand myself, I must recognize myself in other people," says Marco Iacoboni.[4]

So-called "mirror neurons," recently discovered in humans, help us feel what other people are experiencing as if it were happening to us, indicating that we are all connected by "wireless" means, which helps to explain the existence of empathy. The human race is One, a single entity, an enormous family reunion, and our job here is to meet the cousins whom we never see and create larger and larger communities of peace.

Understanding all this prepares us to make the next quantum leap, something that is definitely foreign to Christian theology. If we are part of God, if our consciousness is a sliver of God's consciousness, then, since God has no beginning, we have existed as part of Him forever, since before the beginning of time. We are as eternal as God. I don't know how you can avoid this conclusion. The only counter argument is that we are part of a special creation, but that implies that there is something else out of which God could make us. And there *is* nothing else. Creation is part of God. Period!

If we have existed from the beginning with God, what have we been doing all this time? Let me ask the opposite question. If, as Christians believe, we came from nothingness into life at the moment of our conception, and if we go to heaven at death, having lived this one lifetime, what do we do for eternity? The church avoids this question because it has no answer. The only thing it can suggest is that we sit on a cloud playing a harp, praising God for eternity. Is that really what God created us for, to live on Earth for one little blip in eternity, and then to have nothing to do forever after? I believe that God values us enough to plan something a little more productive than that!

If we have been made in God's image, with His creative drive and His wisdom, then we must conclude that we are here to maximize our potential. God gives us the opportunity to grow, to mature, to gain spiritual wisdom – in other words, to become like Jesus. Jesus made it clear that we would do greater things than he did,[5] which certainly implies a process of growth and accomplishment on our part. This kind of profound wisdom is not attained in a single lifetime on Earth, or even a dozen. Jesus was a highly evolved soul, and he obviously expects us to evolve in the same way. But we can accumulate that kind of knowledge and wisdom only by experiencing a great many lifetimes.

We have the opportunity to live countless lives, but we are not required to do so. The gift of free will is granted to us in heaven as well as on Earth. Some will choose not to accept the hard work of incarnating, just as many of us here do not choose to work at improving our mind or situation. But if we do, we have some degree of input about the circumstances into which we will be born. We can choose our parents, our sex, and other details of our human existence. People have spoken about their pre-birth period, during which they were very much involved in their future mother's pregnancy. A healthy body is of great importance to the soul preparing for entrance into physical life. On the other hand, we may choose some form of physical or mental limitation, in order to learn specific skills and to experience a certain kind of interaction with others. This could be a karmic choice which would help to balance some unsatisfactory performance in a former life. Also, we tend to incarnate in groups so as to examine all aspects of our relationships with a particular set of souls. So in my next life, I might switch sex and become the daughter of my current son during his next incarnation.

We might note here, parenthetically, that the nonsense about being punished by coming back as a bug, or some other undesirable creature, is merely proof that other religions also have their own myths. This is a Buddhist version of the Boogie Man, a story with which to frighten children into being good. There are various types of created beings, all equally valuable in God's sight – animals, humans, angels, etc. Since angels are a different class of created being, distinct from our spirit type, we don't become angels, and angels do not incarnate. By the same token, since animals are a different type of creation, we don't become animals, and vice versa.[6]

Reincarnation answers many of the questions to which religion has no satisfactory response. The primary one has to do with the inequality of the human condition, with some people living in splendor while others are reduced to the worst kind of poverty. Does God love some of us more than others? This is obviously not true.

In John 9:2, the disciples ask Jesus a very interesting question. They are discussing why a certain man had been blind from birth, and they ask, *"Teacher, whose sin caused him to be born blind? Was it his own or his parents' sin?"* The clear implication here is that, if the man was being punished for his own sins, those sins had to have been committed in a former life. And the disciples seem to accept this, understanding that the inequalities in life are caused by the karmic histories of the people involved; that is, our previous lifetimes generate conditions which are reflected in our current life, for good or bad.

This is a far more satisfying way to think about it than to say that our circumstances are the result of mere chance, and that social inequalities have no moral component – some people are just born lucky and others are born unlucky. That makes no sense at all. Understanding karma makes us responsible for our own situation, and removes from God the accusation of gross unfairness. It also provides us with an incentive to improve our own life and the lives of those around us, rather than thinking that this is a dog-eat-dog world in which what I do to others has no consequences for me.

There is no hell, aside from the ones we create for ourselves. The idea of God creating an eternal fiery furnace was thought up by people who had a grudge against others and who imagined for them the worst possible form of punishment. God loves us as part of Himself, and He did not create us so that He could torture us eternally for crimes committed in this little sliver of time. We don't punish for a lifetime a child who steals a penny at age four. God does not punish for eternity a crime committed in the dimension of time. If Gilbert and Sullivan's Mikado knew that a humane punishment should fit the crime and not be out of proportion to it, we can assume that God abides by the same principle. That is why He has created the concept of karma, the law of balance: to achieve equilibrium.

Jesus made it clear that what we do to others will be done to us. Those who pray the Lord's Prayer enter into a karmic contract with God: they ask God to forgive them only as much as they forgive others. Karma works both ways: it can be a reward for things lovingly done, and it can be the consequence of negative behavior. Karma is not punishment, but a way of seeing why a certain action is wrong and hurtful, and in that way it becomes a means of bringing things back into balance.

A simple example might be that a person who commits a murder in one life is himself murdered in the next life, to bring about closure and achieve balance and understanding. Or a person who risks his life for another might find a friend in the next life who is willing to protect him with his own life. Karma is educational, not punitive. God is not interested in punishing us; He wants us to gain wisdom. Burning us forever in hell would do little to make us any wiser.

We come here with a specific task in mind, something which will increase our wisdom or compensate for some destructive behavior in a previous existence. What we are doing is important to God. In a sense, we are a piece of God which He sends out to increase His own knowledge and power. As we grow, He grows, and vice versa. God may well be the accumulation in one consciousness of all the awareness of all the sentient beings in the history of the universe. And much more.

So, in order to accomplish the goal for which we came, we are provided with personal spiritual aides whose job it is to support and assist us in our earthly task. They are both angels and spirit guides. Angels, as we have said, do not incarnate. Spirit guides, on the other hand, may have been human in the past, and may well be friends who have volunteered to be our guide in this lifetime.

In one of my study groups, we came up with a mental picture which helped us visualize our connection to our guides. We saw ourselves as deep sea divers, lowered into the ocean of physical reality, with the surface of the Earth serving as the ocean floor. This is alien territory for us, since we are residents of heaven. Therefore, we are encased in our protective diving suits – our physical bodies – which make it possible for us to survive in this hostile environment.

But this is not something we can do alone. Without having air pumped down to us, we would die in minutes. That is the responsibility of the guides. They remain in a boat on the surface of this ocean, faithfully pumping away to supply us not only with air but with love and life. We cannot live without being sustained from above.

I believe this is why we are asleep for a full third of our lives. God could have made us so we need only an hour of sleep a night, or no sleep at all, but He created us to be unconscious for half as long as we are awake. Why? Because, I believe, during those eight hours nightly while our body is asleep, we get hauled up from the ocean bottom, leaving our hard suits behind, and we climb back into the boat with our guides. There we consult and get instructions on how to conduct our explorations the next day. We need that nightly conference to remind us of our spiritual identity, and to learn new skills which will make us more successful in our earthly mission. Some of our dreams are merely distorted memories of those encounters, because the actual event cannot fit into our three-dimensional awareness. When we don't get our full eight hours a night, we are not just sleep-deprived; we are spirit-deprived, which is why it makes us a little crazy!

Since God is pure spirit and not a person, He recognizes the need to reach out to us in a form with which we can easily connect. When a little boy told his mother that he was afraid of the dark when he went to bed, she said that God would watch over him. He protested, "But I want a God with skin on his face." The angels and our spirit guides – as well as Jesus himself – are the skin on God's face, the beings who turn God from pure power into an entity with whom we can identify and interact.

13

So, to summarize, our natural environment is the spirit world in the presence of God. We are all a part of God, and thus are related to each other. We elect to come here to use physical life as a form of school, and our choices about the conditions and purpose of our life are based on our previous karmic record. For instance, if we fail math during the school year, we might decide to take a remedial math course in summer school. Or, conversely, if we aced the math course during the year, we might be asked to help teach the remedial course. The purpose of life is to balance failures and benefit from successes on our way to spiritual transcendence. Death is merely the moment when our physical body ceases to function, at which point our spirit reverts to the spiritual world from whence it came.

The Judgment Day that the church warns us about is a self-judgment. In the presence of God's love, we have the opportunity to review a "film" of our recent lifetime, in which we are able to see both our behavior and its effects on other people. On the basis of this, and after a period of rest, reflection and further instruction, we are free to plan our next excursion into the physical, in an attempt to balance the things we observed in our past life review.

The dire warnings of hell and damnation with which the church threatens us are, as you can see, mostly unjustified. It does not matter which religion we belong to. We are not kept out of "heaven" because we are "bad." We do not have to wait for a "second coming" to be resurrected, since we instantly return to spirit at the moment of death. Our inter-life period involves rest and study in preparation for the next lifetime. We are eternal spirits, and our consciousness has been given to us for the purpose of growth, with the goal of transcendence. We strive to become more like Jesus so that we can become more like the God from whom we originate. There are those who believe that God is creating for Himself a consort, equal in wisdom and creative potential to Himself, and that you and I are cells in this developing spiritual organism.

Everything in life and death has meaning, and all of it is good, as judged by God. In the end we will see the purpose of it all, and be amazed at God's good plan.

Chapter Three

Myth and Religion

Two young siblings sneak downstairs on Christmas morning while their parents are still asleep. The kids behold the age-old panorama – a Christmas tree with piles of colorful packages beneath it, alongside a table on which stands a glass half full of warm milk and a cookie with teeth marks in it. The little boy says to his big sister, "Tell me again where all these presents come from." So his sister sits him down and begins.

"Santa Claus lives at the North Pole, and he and his elves spend the whole year building toys for all the boys and girls. Then, on Christmas Eve, he puts the toys in his sleigh, hooks up his eight reindeer – and sometimes Rudolph, too – and flies around the world in one night. He stops at every house, lands on the roof, slides down the chimney with his bulging sack, puts toys under the tree for the good boys and girls, and a lump of coal in the stockings of the naughty ones. Then he slides back up the chimney and goes on to the next house."

That story summons up an interesting comparison. Two adults are talking, one a Christian and the other an unbeliever. The agnostic says, "Tell me again what it is that you believe." So the churchgoer sits him down and begins.

"God created the human race, and He wants everyone to be with Him in heaven. But we are all so sinful and depraved that we are not worthy to be in God's presence. So He created a plan by which He could make us good enough to be with Him for eternity. He took on human form and became a man named Jesus, who came to earth and walked among us for thirty-three years. He told people how to be

15

accepted by God, and performed many miracles – he walked on water, turned water into wine, healed the sick and raised the dead. But religious people didn't like what he was doing, so they killed him by nailing him to a cross. However, God raised him from the dead, brought him back to life and took him up to heaven in his physical body. Now, everyone who believes that Jesus was the son of God will go to heaven. But those who don't believe in him, and the people who lived before Jesus, and those from other religions, will all go to hell where Satan will throw them into a fire of brimstone and burn them forever. This shows how much God loves those who believe in Jesus, and how much He hates those who don't."

There are interesting similarities between these two narratives. Both are fanciful explanations of something ineffable – human love in the first case and divine love in the second. Both are wonderful traditional concepts, but both are nothing more than metaphors. Santa is a symbol of the love we have for each other, and Jesus is a symbol of God's love for all of us. But regardless of how much we love the Santa story, no thinking adult takes it literally. It is obvious to rational minds that it's a myth. Those who do take it literally are either children or intellectually deficient. And yet a great proportion of the world's people see the Jesus story as literal fact.

We began by defining "myth" as "a story of ostensibly historical events that serves to unfold part of the world view of a people." For purposes of this book, we could define religion with the same words. But we are aware that while the story may be ostensibly historical, it is not literal fact; it is myth. We have to be clear, however, that a myth is not the same as untruth. Myth functions as truth on a metaphorical level: it expresses a subjective truth in imaginative terms. But it is still a symbol rather than a statement of objective reality.

If we were to hear the Jesus story today about someone from our own time, we would react far differently. Suppose the church began to preach the good news that Walter Cronkite, the most trusted newsman of his time, was really a savior sent from God, that he walked on water and healed the sick, that he was killed by bad people but was miraculously brought back to life, and that we have to worship him or go to hell. We would dismiss such a claim as lunacy.

While good news of this sort might well have been believable 2,000 years ago to that uneducated and superstitious Middle Eastern public, we would rightly see such a claim about Cronkite today as preposterous. Yet, because the Jesus story has been taught for 2,000 years, because it is built into the fabric of the world's greatest religious empire, and because so many people continue to believe it today, that story has been grandfathered into our modern philosophical worldview. We are taught to suspend our disbelief and embrace it as truth, even though we would reject out of hand such a story if it were to arise in today's world.

Most Christians were born into their religion rather than having been converted. This means that it is an inherited faith rather than one which has been chosen after careful thought and study. And in my experience as a pastor, most people never question how their religion began. They look at the church buildings which dot their town, they think back on the religious practices of their parents and grandparents, they see the pope on television addressing his millions of fellow Roman Catholics, they participate in Christmas and Easter celebrations, and they never question the authenticity of the Christian faith. The sheer momentum of this faith tradition is as ponderous and unstoppable as a glacier. Can two billion human beings be wrong?

Well, no...and yes. They are not wrong in believing what the church says about the *existence* of God. They are wrong when they accept what the church says about the *nature* of God. It is metaphor, picturesque imagery which attempts to describe the indescribable. In other words – myth.

We need to think here about how a religion is formed. No religion has existed from the beginning of time. There were no Christians anywhere on Earth in the year AD 25. Religion is not dropped intact from heaven. It is invented by human beings in response to some event in their communal lives. And that event gives them a metaphor around which to organize cultic rituals which help define their community.

Earliest man realized that both blessings and threats came from overhead – the sun chased away the dark night with all its unseen threats, the rain made things grow that were essential to life, but storms filled the sky and showed him how powerless he was over his environment, lightning bolts were tossed from heaven and set his world aflame. These things were totally out of his control, but he reasoned that some great power made them happen. So he concluded that there must be super-humans up there with abilities far beyond his own. And those gods should be honored and obeyed so that they would both give the people what they needed and protect them from harm. Thus, these early people developed rituals designed to mollify and befriend the gods of nature.

A marvelous example of this in the present day is the development of Cargo Cults in the south Pacific during World War II. The inhabitants of some of those isolated islands had never seen modern technology before the allied troops invaded their lands to use them as stepping stones to Japan. These foreigners built airfields and flew planes in and out, all the while giving much needed food and supplies to the natives. When the war ended and the military pulled out, the indigenous people were left with a thrilling story to tell succeeding generations: There was a time when they were visited by gods who came from the sky and brought them all kinds of wonderful gifts. So, in an effort to induce those gods to return and continue to shower them with goods, the people developed elaborate rituals which were often conducted around worship centers featuring crudely built images of airplanes.

If asked for a symbol which represented their "religion," they would tell you it was an airplane, two pieces of wood nailed together in a form surprisingly reminiscent of a cross. Their lack of understanding about the source of this aerial visitation led them to invent a myth about what had once happened to them, a myth based on both hope and ignorance. But, in truth, their religious activities had no actual connection to reality, and certainly were ineffective in getting the warplanes to return.

There is an interesting similarity between the Cargo Cults and the beginning of the Christian religion. Some kind of remarkable event happened 2,000 years ago. A man was born in the Middle East who was filled with the spirit of God. He did marvelous things and caused the people to turn to God. After his death, his followers formed a cult around the story of his life. They worshipped him as a god and elaborated the story of his ministry in order to convince others that he had been the very presence of God in their midst.

Again, while this story may well have been based on the life of a real man, its evolution into a world religion has little if any connection with the actual reality of the spirit world. Rather, it is based on human needs and fears. In the same way that primitive man begged the gods for sustenance and protection, we continue to project our desires upward toward heaven. And since God is invisible, the Jesus story conveniently provides God with a face. Nothing much has changed in religion, however, from primitive times to the present. We do the same things religiously that our forefathers did, although in far more splendid spaces. We pray for blessings; We ask for protection from things we fear; We try to gain favor with our god so that he will reward us with heaven; We discipline our behavior for fear that our god might send us to hell.

We have evolved to the point where we can throw our minds to the far ends of the universe and reel them back in filled with unanswerable questions. And we have used our creative imaginations to formulate answers to those unanswerable questions. But those answers are mere speculations; they are created from our need and our fear rather than from any certain knowledge of the other world.

We have to be honest with ourselves about what the human mind is capable of. We can't even answer the most basic question of all: Why am I here? What's the meaning of life? We have tried to invent answers to those questions, but our attempts are as feeble as throwing pebbles at the moon in an effort to change its course. Our minds do not come equipped with the software necessary to understand the spiritual side of existence.

As a result, we have to be honest enough to admit that the answers we have invented to these religious questions are incomplete and ignorant, and that they were never meant to be fixed and final for all time. Each one is a mythological place-holder in our evolutionary journey, meant to keep us focused at the current level until the next series of revelations comes along. And what we need to recognize right now is that we have recently entered a new age of revelation. It is time to take the next step forward in our spiritual knowledge.

The purpose of revelation is to assist us in our spiritual evolution, as we move from primitive myths to an ever more sophisticated understanding of the divine. Each new story we develop about God will still be a myth, but each one will take us a fraction of the distance closer to the truth. Indeed, we have reason to hope that the next level in our spiritual evolution – similar to the moment we crawled out of the water onto dry land – will be the point when we crawl out of the muddy water of our present me-first mentality and find ourselves on the dry land of true God-consciousness. At that point, we will begin to produce human beings who live in the full knowledge of their spiritual nature, who are equally familiar with both worlds, and who will be able to create the long promised Kingdom of God here on Earth. If we are actually evolving spiritually, what other destiny can there be for us?

In the meantime, we have to remember that we are created as three-dimensional beings, and that we cannot, by our nature, conceive of the attributes of God – eternal, infinite, omniscient, omnipresent, omnipotent, spiritual. Therefore, the god we invent looks a lot more like ourselves than like God. At this point, we are incapable of creating anything but myths, because our minds are too small to comprehend the vast truth of God. Attempting to cram God's 100-dimensional reality into our 3-dimensional brains is about as successful as trying to cut down a California redwood with a nail file. As a result, while children describe God as a very old man with a long white beard, our adult images are not a whole lot more accurate. But each of these evolutionary steps brings us closer to God, and reminds us that we are spiritual beings answerable to a higher power. It is essential, therefore, to allow these mythological images of God constantly to evolve and grow.

In the Bible, we can see a perfect example of this evolutionary process in humanity's thinking about God. Compare the images of God found in the two testaments. The God of the Old Testament is a warlike god who commands His people to slaughter His enemies. It takes little imagination to see that the Israelites merely projected their national prejudices onto God, and thus justified their violent behavior against their neighbors by claiming that God had commanded them to do it. By the time we get to the New Testament, however, Jesus is teaching us to call God "Abba," which translates something like "Daddy." A far different image. There is a process at work here, and it did not stop with the completion of the New Testament. When Jesus said that he had more to tell us, he made it clear that this evolution in our spiritual understanding is to continue into our own time and beyond.

But the problem is that the church's myth, for the most part, has not changed and evolved. The ancient Christian image of the Almighty's plan has been set in concrete for centuries and worshiped as the final word from on high. The church continues to hang on to its primitive concepts of spiritual reality which, though they may be well-intentioned, are far from the truth. Those ideas do not represent an accurate portrayal of the interaction between the physical and spiritual worlds.

We can understand why the church is so reluctant to change, but we cannot allow that to be an excuse for failing to listen to the new revelations. The church is defined by its doctrine, and it has to defend the orthodoxy of these teachings or lose its identity. But, how is the church to know which new discoveries are legitimate and which should be guarded against? It is far easier to move forward with a fixed doctrine inscribed on stone tablets than to pray for the Spirit to illuminate each forward step to be taken. There is always the chance that we might be wrong. But the alternative is for the church to become totally irrelevant, and for the future of spirituality to find its home in some entirely new institution.

Furthermore, since we are each anchored in our own distinctive culture, each traditional myth about the divine will take on the social aspects and tribal practices of the group which has developed it. There are many different religious stories in use among the world's people at the same time, each one pointing to the same deity, yet each one differing in significant details from the rest.

As a result, we can see the utter nonsense of any group claiming that its god, its theology, its religious myth is the only true one and that all others are false and their people destined for hell. That kind of thinking ultimately leads to a belief that all those who think differently than we do are enemies of God, and that getting rid of them will meet with God's favor. Religious intolerance of this sort is a prime example of how religion has failed.

Until we realize that there is nothing but God – that we are all part of the same God and therefore part of one another, and that what we do to others we do to ourselves – until that day, there will be no peace on earth. Religion leads us away from this goal because it focuses on who is saved and who is damned. In doing so, it accomplishes the opposite of what it claims as its mission – it brings a sword rather than a plowshare. The Kingdom of God comes from spiritual oneness, not from the divisiveness caused by taking literally the various myths we call religion.

Here's one more illustration of the problem caused by thinking of myth as literal truth. Two children are talking. One asks the other where babies come from. The other lifts his shirt and points to his navel. "They pop out of a mommy's bellybutton." The first child asks in surprise, "How can that happen?" And the child, with all the authority of a five-year-old, says, "Her belly gets real big and so does her belly button, and when it's time for the baby to be born, she sneezes and the baby pops out!"

This is a reasonable kindergarten view of that mysterious process, and does not surprise us. It is a myth invented by a child who has not yet learned the truth. But what if his parents had told him that this *was* the truth, that babies do pop out of bellybuttons, and what if all of his friends were told the same thing, and what if all the literature in the field said that it was true, in spite of the daily evidence that such a tale was nonsense? We would think that parents who told their children repeated lies about the matter, perhaps because they had also been lied to in their own childhood, were doing their children great harm.

Yet, well-meaning parents pass on to their children all the mythological stories that they learned in Sunday School – that Jesus walked on water, turned water into wine, rose from the dead, and ascended into heaven in his physical body. And they do this in spite of all we know about science. Babies do not pop out of navels, and God does not walk around in a human disguise.

The only way to free the next generations from this primitive theology is to recognize that these stories are simple ways to describe the love of God. They are myth; they are not literal history. Responsible parents pick a time to sit down with their children and quietly explode the myth of Santa Clause and the Easter bunny. They need to do the same thing with the Christian story. When we do that, we can begin to understand the deeper truth that this ancient story is attempting to communicate, and we can move a step closer to God.

How can we relate to God when so much of what we have been told about Him is a distortion? The God of religious tradition does not exist. The God of the spirit world is much greater than what we have been taught. God's revelation about Himself is continuing, and we need to cooperate with each other in creating ever larger and more accurate myths.

Chapter Four

Salvation

We Don't Need A Savior.

I can imagine how shocking that statement is to some good church members. After all, isn't having a savior – being saved – what religion is all about? The Bible tells us in Romans 3:23-25:

Everyone has sinned and is far away from God's saving presence. But by the free gift of God's grace all are put right with him through Christ Jesus, who sets them free. God offered him, so that by his blood he should become the means by which people's sins are forgiven through their faith in him.

And Romans 6:23:

For sin pays its wage – death; but God's free gift is eternal life in union with Christ Jesus our Lord.

So we are told that we are corrupt sinners, that left to ourselves our only future is spiritual death. Therefore, we must be redeemed; we need at-*one*ment, some act which reconnects us with God and makes us one with Him. Otherwise we will never be acceptable to Him and will face eternal punishment.

Then scripture goes on to tell us that there is an escape hatch: faith in Jesus' death and resurrection. The religion which sprang up around those events tells us that if we do what the church fathers tell us to do, we can escape the fiery destiny which God has planned for us. Without the fear of hellfire, there would be no purpose for religion. The main message of the church is this: Jesus died on the cross to save us from our sins. He is our savior. Without him we cannot be saved from damnation. There is no other way to heaven.

Well, I'm here with the effrontery to tell you that this is not true. Remember, *religion is based on myth*, so the story about our needing a savior to keep us out of hell is also…myth.

I love the church and what I have to say here is not meant to be offensive, but I have to tell you, as a former pastor, that the church leadership can become addicted to power. The Bible exerts power over the church; the church hierarchy exerts power over the clergy; the clergy inherits that power in its ordination and uses it to tell the people what is true and what is not. There is an insidious self-importance that comes with the commission to tell people what they can and can't do. The right to threaten people with hell as a means of controlling their behavior has tempted many a pastor to lose his humility and his humanity.

The source of the clergy's power is what's written in The Book and stated in the church's confessions of faith. Therefore, the clergy has a vested interest in defending that system of doctrine because it defines who they are and legitimizes their power. If their ancient story were suddenly shown to be untrue, they would instantly be stripped of their authority, and thus they would lose the power to control the lives of their communicants.

Now, not all clergy are as overt in their exercise of power as this might sound, but the subtle effect of their religious authority is a factor in everything they do. This is apparent in the way many lay people treat clergy members, as a group set apart, to be treated with a deference that somehow comes with their collar. They call them "Reverend" or "Father," which automatically puts distance between them; they apologize for swearing in their presence (which has always amused me since "hell" and "damn" are part of the clergyman's professional vocabulary!) And as long as the clergy preaches that there is divine punishment for human misbehavior, they maintain a powerful whip to crack over the heads of their people – the fear of God. If you don't think that this inflates clerical egos, you need to take a closer look. Try to take that power away from them and you will hear an enormous outcry. Even suggest that the story which gives them their power might not be true, and they will summon the troops and accuse you of working for the devil.

That whole damnation/salvation belief is nothing more than an ancient holdover reflecting the power that royalty once exerted over its people. Those who developed the church's early theology could think of nothing to compare God with except earthly kings and their unlimited power. So they attributed to God all the attributes of royalty which they both admired and feared – the power of life and death, of punishment and reward. That power was ultimately conferred upon the clergy. The common understanding in the church has been that the religious hierarchy knows the truth about God and the people don't. Therefore, it's the job of the clergy to preach the truth, and the duty of the laity to listen and obey. And the clergy, which once literally held the power of life and death over believers, symbolically retains that power in the right to excommunicate those who fail to follow the church's teaching, killing their souls by consigning them to hell.

The laity, for its part, plays right along with this religious game. Most people are uncertain about these things, frightened of the unknown, and they're glad to have someone who will tell them what to do. They don't want to spend a lot of time thinking about such things because they're busy with their lives, but at the same time they don't want to make a mistake which will end them up in hell simply because they forgot one little jot or tittle of the law. So the church fathers obligingly step up and say, "We will be that source of authority for you. We know secrets that you could never know because you are only ignorant pew sitters."

Of course, the clergy doesn't know any more about heaven than Pete the Plumber does. But no one wants to argue with them because they have a habit of saying, "Don't mess with me because I speak for God, and messing with me is messing with God. And you don't want to be caught doing that!" I know this is true because I spent forty years behind a pulpit raised above the heads of the congregation, a neat little trick which subtly made them look up to me.

The church has always had this alluring little contract with its people – do what we say and we'll guarantee that you'll get into heaven. At one point during the Middle Ages, some church people believed that they could buy indulgences from the church that promised to shorten the time they or their loved ones had to spend in purgatory. That practice suggested that the church had extraordinary control over what happens in heaven! The Bible even confirms this when it claims that Jesus said to Peter:

"I will give you the keys of the Kingdom of heaven; what you prohibit on earth will be prohibited in heaven, and what you permit on earth will be permitted in heaven." [7]

So, in other words, at least one human being can tell God what to do – who to accept and who to reject. Who wouldn't want to be part of an institution which has this kind of pull with the Almighty?

The problem is, it's not true.

When I say that we don't need a savior, how should I expect the church to respond? A savior – that is, a kind of divine fire insurance – is the chief commodity that the church is selling. When we try to say that it's unnecessary, it threatens to put them out of business. So of course they're going to object. Strenuously! It's like the emperor's new clothes. If we expose their game, they're going to look foolish running around naked without their robes and miters.

We are spiritual beings. We are embodied spirits. We are a two-part invention of God, a soul which will last forever inside a body which will decay after seven or eight decades. So, our true nature is God's nature, not the world's nature. We belonged to God long before we belonged to the church. Our contract with God is not through the church or the priest or the pope. Our contract is directly with God. We are intended to be our own priest!

The reformers in the 16th century made a stab at this truth by proclaiming "the priesthood of all believers" in an attempt to get around the authority of the clergy. But even they were concerned about the implications of letting each believer think for himself. As a result, that whole concept has never been taken seriously in the church. If it really were to be taken at face value, people might discover that this whole church business is unnecessary. And, of course, the authorities couldn't let that happen! Power, as we have noted, is very addictive.

The fact is, there is nothing but God. When we say that God is the creator, we mean *nothing* that exists was created by any means other than the will and the mind of God. We don't know why or how this happened, but our new spiritual worldview tells us that the universe and everything in it is part of God, part of the substance and the essence of God. And if God is perfect, then every item which He has created is perfect. And that includes us!

Therefore...if God is perfect, and everything He made is perfect, and if therefore we are perfect in God's eyes – in spite of being imperfect in our own – what, pray tell, do we need to be saved from? God doesn't think we need saving. We're part of Himself, and God is not going to condemn and disown a part of His own being. But, you say, it's obvious that we are not perfect, and nothing imperfect can come into the presence of God. And this is true. But when we appear before God, He doesn't see a sinner. He sees only a person who is loved with an infinite and unqualified love.

But at the same time, that person may bring with him the memory of certain actions and failures which we think of as sin. Yet, what we see as the conflict between sin and righteousness, God sees in a different light. For God, there is only what works and what doesn't work. And we have chosen to become human for the purpose of discovering the difference between those two values.

What we call sin God sees as one more thing that doesn't work in our lives. Did Edison's thousands of unsuccessful attempts to create a light bulb qualify as failures? Of course not. Each one of those experiments netted him another bit of wisdom. "Well," he could say, "that's one more thing I can cross off my list of possible solutions." Each unsuccessful attempt cannot be termed a failure because each one brought him that much closer to the final success.

The same thing is true of our efforts to discover what works in the process of learning the joy of true spirituality. We have to try everything to see what works. We try murder. Nope, that doesn't work. Too expensive for me and for everyone else. We might try drugs. Nope, that doesn't work either because it ruins my consciousness along with ravaging my body. We try casual sex, and end up lonely and isolated from true relationships. We try power and money and find that there is an emptiness inside us that *things* can't fill. Step by step we approach God as we try, and then discard, the things that don't work. The goal is joy, wisdom, the kindling of an inner light, and one by one we mark off the things that work against that desired outcome. It may take many lifetimes to get there, but that is why we have been given eternity in which to conduct this quest. Life is a matter of accumulating the things that work, and letting go of the things that don't.

The process by which a child learns to walk is a telling metaphor for this. How do we learn to walk? By falling down! No child walks flawlessly the first time he or she makes the attempt. Falling down is an important element in learning how to achieve balance. Is each fall a failure? Not if you see it as a step toward success. Only if you cannot see the larger picture do you consider it a failure. Do loving parents punish their child every time he or she falls down while learning to walk? Of course not. They are thrilled that the child has reached the stage where they are ready to take the next step in their development. Every fall is a move forward and eventually, after many falls, the child learns to walk confidently.

Then what happens? The child continues to test himself/herself. Having learned to walk, they try running, and fall down many more times in the process. When they learn to run, they try hopping, walking on curbs, jumping over barriers, and each new skill comes with its own set of falls. But each fall is a new lesson, and eventually the skills are learned.

God, as our loving parent, sees what we call our sins as falls on our way to learning the most important skill of all, walking in spiritual transcendence. In the same way that our parents did not punish us for our falls but encouraged us to get up and try again, so God does not punish us. He gives us all the time we need to perfect our skills. The biblical word for sin means to miss the mark, as we do in archery when we hit something other than the bullseye. What God wants us to do is to improve our aim, and it is foolish to think that burning us in hell for eternity is going to do much for our archery skills.

Well, you say, does this mean there is no sin, no misbehavior that deserves punishment or retribution, no limits on what people are allowed to do? Does God accept everything we do and merely wink at our destructive behavior? We know all too well that there are crimes of all types in this world. We want justice, and merely saying that God loves us is not justice.

The answer to that question is simple and logical. Because God is perfect, His justice and righteousness are also perfect. And the solution God has come up with is this: We are punished *by* our sins, not *for* them. When children fall on the way to walking, we don't punish them, but they may inadvertently hurt themselves. Learning these developmental skills can be, and often is, a painful process. There are many tears shed along the route to accomplishment because the accumulation of skills is inherently painful.

In the same way, our road to transcendence is a painful one, since every fall entails its own "punishment." God does not spank us when we "sin." God lets us suffer the consequences of our fall, and that is punishment enough. We don't learn from a stick that is applied externally; that only teaches us resentment and anger. We learn from the pain that we inflict on ourselves. The most mature thing we can say in this process is, "Well, I guess I won't do *that* again!" We have to learn these things for ourselves. Not even God can teach them to us. And what we learn from our own pain is stored up in our personal library of wisdom.

The word for this process is – Karma.

We will spend more time talking about this later on. But let us at this point repeat the statement with which we began this chapter. We Don't Need A Savior. If this assertion is true, what does it do to the central message of the Christian religion? It makes it null and void. And without that single teaching – that we need a savior who is available only through religion - the entire tradition falls apart. That is, *unless we can finally agree that religion is a myth.*

When that day finally dawns, the faith of our fathers will take on a bright new metaphorical meaning, and will come alive with riches to give every one of us. I believe sincerely that this was what Jesus had in mind from the very beginning. He had no intention of starting a new religion. He just told parables about the Kingdom of God. But the biggest parable of all is the one which his followers created, the religion of Jesus. When we begin to treat it the same way as we treat the parable of the Good Samaritan – that it never really happened but that it has valuable things to teach us – then we will enter a brand new age of spiritual awareness.

Chapter Five

The Bible

The Bible Is Not the Word of God

If we're going to make our case that Christianity is based on a myth, we have to look at the documents which support it to determine how reliable they are.

Let me begin by asking a question: How many animals of each kind did Noah take onto the ark with him? If I told you that he took on board fourteen of certain animals, what would you think? You might well say that I hadn't read my Bible very carefully. Everyone knows that Noah took *one* pair of each kind of animal onto the ark. "What about the old Sunday School song?" you might ask: "The animals entered two-by-two, the elephant and the kangaroo."

Well, I would say that you should go back and read the story more carefully. In Genesis 7:2-3, it says, *"Take with you seven pairs of each kind of ritually clean animal, but only one pair of each kind of unclean animal. Take also seven pairs of each kind of bird."*

Then in 7:7-9 it says, *"[Noah]...went into the boat to escape the flood. A male and a female of every kind of animal and bird, whether ritually clean or unclean, went into the boat with Noah, as God had commanded."*

Whoa! Now, wait a minute. We have a bit of a problem here. Was Noah commanded to take two or fourteen of each kind of animal with him? Did God change the instructions between verses 2 and 7 as to how many ritually clean animals were to be included? Or is this whole passage merely an effort to confuse poor old Noah?

Well, it's clear that God didn't command Noah to do either one. What we have here are two different versions of an ancient myth, variations of the same story which were passed down by different tribal elements of the same culture. So, rather than this passage being dictated by God, we see it as a piece of the mythological history of the Hebrew people. And they didn't even bother to get the details to agree!

Look at some of the other parts of the story. The water covered the highest mountains (7:19). In fact, it was about twenty-five feet above the tops of the mountains (7:20). This means that the entire planet was totally submerged. No land at all. Think about how much water that would require. Certainly more than a constant rainfall of forty days could supply (7:17), even including *"the vast body of water beneath the earth"* (7:11). Then we are told that the rain stopped and, after the water went down for 150 days, the ark came to rest on a mountain in the Ararat range (8:4). And yet, the tops of the mountains didn't appear for another three months! (8:5) Then, only a couple of months after that, when Noah had turned 601 years old, the Earth was completely dry. Where had all that water gone? There were no oceans for it to run off into because the whole world was one big ocean!

Add to this the incredible effort involved in rounding up each of the world's animals, and then trying to wedge them all into the same small boat. And finally, consider a god who could be angry enough with his creation to kill all his children. Some would say that the whole story, with all its discrepancies, is a miracle. But it's obviously a myth, and as such is not to be taken literally.

So, that raises the question: how much of the rest of the Bible is myth and not literal history? Since it's in the Bible, some people insist that the Noah story actually happened. There are flood myths in many different cultures, so there was certainly some ancient event on which these tales were based. But to expand the story from some local catastrophe to a worldwide inundation is to turn history into myth. And this kind of process can be seen in many places in scripture.

Look at the creation story in Genesis 1. It is clear, according to the narrative, that God created not just the world but the whole universe in six days (2:1). We know of course that this is not true, but there are those who are convinced that it is, simply because the Bible says it is. This is the worst side effect of biblical literalism; it causes people to believe things which we know are nonsense from a scientific point of view. Religion should not dispute the facts. If God made the facts, religion needs to embrace them, regardless of whether they agree with the Bible or not.

An interesting thing to note in the creation story is that God created light and darkness, day and night on the first day. But he didn't get around to creating the sun and the moon until the fourth day (1:14-19). How does that work?! This story is a beautiful tribute to the creator of the universe, but that doesn't change the fact that it is a primitive and unsophisticated account of creation. To demand that it be taught to our children as objective truth is intellectually dishonest.

In Genesis 2:3 it says that God rested on the seventh day and set it apart as a holy day. The word Sabbath means *rest* and refers to the last day of the Jewish calendar, *Shabbat*. Most Jews observe it in obedience to the command in this passage of scripture. What interested me as a Christian minister was how that idea was appropriated by conservative Christians who were determined to shackle the Christian holy day with all the restrictions of the Old Testament Sabbath. I grew up in a Christian family with a grandfather who was an old-school Presbyterian minister. When we visited him, we were not allowed to play, go to the movies, swim or even cook on the "Christian Sabbath." Food had to be prepared the day before, and children were required to sit quietly and read the Bible or pursue some other sedentary activity.

The irony is that the Sabbath was intended to be *Saturday*, the last day of the week. By contrast, Sunday, the first day of the week, is more appropriately called The Lord's Day rather than the Sabbath. Sunday is an entirely different kind of observance because it is a celebration of the resurrection, which happened on Sunday. The Lord's Day was intended as a day of joy and freedom, not an occasion to reapply the Jewish law from which the Good News of the Gospel was supposed to have set us free. Nevertheless, I always had people in my church who insisted on referring to Sunday classes as Sabbath School. Isn't it interesting how adherence to the Bible can produce distortions like this which actually work to counteract the truths which religion is supposed to teach?

The Bible contains a number of things which we should reject today. For instance, I Cor. 14:35 reads, *"It is a disgraceful thing for a woman to speak in a church meeting."* Paul declares, in verse 34, *"Women should keep quiet in the meetings. They are not allowed to speak: as the Jewish Law says, they must not be in charge."* Apparently Paul hadn't heard that Jesus came to introduce a new dispensation, to *free* us from the old Jewish law. But he was unable to shake off his early training. As a result, he felt that all the bigotry and sexism of the Old Testament should become part of the new Christian religion.

So, the church is still one of the worst examples of institutional sexism. Throughout history, it has been a leading anti-feminist force in society because of its need to take everything in the Bible literally. How can we delude ourselves into thinking that, because we call it a holy book, everything in the Bible should be followed slavishly? Many of the things in the Bible are based on the ignorant thought patterns of a primitive time in human development, and yet we feel compelled to honor them today. That behavior is as ignorant as a doctor would be if he read an ancient medical text and then bled a patient because that was what physicians did hundreds of years ago. We don't base modern society on medical and legal texts written in the Middle Ages. Why do we allow our modern quest for spirituality to be guided by writings which are thousands of years out of date?

God certainly isn't prejudiced against women. So it's pretty hard to claim that He dictated these portions of scripture. The Bible is just another human product which, although it is filled with insights into the divine, is also framed by the prejudices and limitations of the human mind.

In Exodus 21:20-21, the Bible clearly states that a slave is the property of his master. It goes on to say that the master can kill his slave without being punished for it, provided that the slave doesn't die for a day or two after the beating!

I Peter 2:18 commands: *"You servants must submit yourselves to your masters and show them complete respect, not only to those who are kind and considerate, but also to those who are harsh."*

Ephesians 6:5: *"Slaves, obey your human masters with fear and trembling; and do it with a sincere heart, as though you were serving Christ."*

I Timothy 6:1: *"Those who are slaves must consider their masters worthy of all respect, so that no one will speak evil of the name of God and of our teaching."*

So the Bible is definitely not anti-slavery. Should we hold slaves today because the Bible condones the practice? You can bet that people in the South before the Civil War used these verses to justify their ownership and treatment of slaves.

In Joshua 11:6, God is quoted as saying, *"Do not be afraid of [your enemies]. By this time tomorrow I will have killed all of them for Israel."*

Exodus 21:7 reads: *"If a man sells his daughter as a slave, she is not to be set free, as male slaves are."*

Deuteronomy 21:18-21 tells us to take a rebellious son to the leaders of the town who will stone him to death as a punishment for his disobedience to his parents.

Exodus 21:15-17 says that anyone who hits or curses his father or his mother is to be put to death.

And we could go on, but I think you get the point. God did not command any of these things. They – along with the relegation of women to second class status and the proscription against homosexuality – are examples of social behaviors of that long ago time which were defended by the claim that they were part of the law of God. But the God about whom Jesus preached has a much higher law, the law of love.

So if God did not say these things, what other things that are recorded in the Bible did God not say? And again, if large portions of scripture did not come from the mind of God, how can we still claim that this is God's Word? *We can't!* The concept of the Bible as God's

Word is one more myth that we have to deal with. We need to let the Holy Spirit guide us through scripture to find those truths which *do* come from God, but we can no longer claim that the whole book is equally inspired, equally sacred.

It's interesting to note that of the sixty-nine books in the Protestant Bible,[8] only four record the life and teachings of the man who is called the Christ. That's only 6% of the entire book. The rest is historical preparation for the coming of the Christ, or post-resurrection commentary on his teachings along with documents pertaining to the church which was formed in his memory.

The Apostle Paul wrote thirteen of these books, three times as many as the books dealing with the life of Jesus. Paul was a member of the Pharisees, a legalistic Jewish sect. He, as much as anyone, is responsible for the development of the Christian religion. He was a missionary who founded numerous local churches. His writings to this day are the basis on which Christian theology is formed. Jesus didn't leave any writings behind, but Paul more than made up for it. As a result, we have paid more attention to what Paul said than to what Jesus said. And this has been disastrous for the Good News of the Gospel. So, rather than "Christianity," the religion should be called "Paulinism." It is Paul's thinking that forms the basic structure of the Christian belief system.

The teachings of Jesus are far different from what Paul taught. Paul found it much easier to return to the structure and legal demands of his Jewish background than to accept the freedom and grace that Jesus preached. Jesus did not come to begin a new religion. His message was radically different. He was saying, in effect, that religion serves one purpose, to prepare people for the coming of the Kingdom of God. But he was preaching that the Kingdom *has already come*, that it is all around us, that we are living in the midst of it. Therefore, since the Kingdom is here, we no longer have to prepare for it. That means that the time for religion is past! Now what we need to do is to live in the Kingdom and celebrate the presence of God in our midst.

Paul, however, with his legalistic background, couldn't understand this message. The only way he knew how to be spiritual

38

was to be religious. He could deal with Jesus' new message only by wrapping it up in the old forms with which he was familiar. So the religion he invented can be described as Judaism wrapped in New Testament language. Jesus would have been horrified. This was the direct opposite of what he hoped his disciples would do.

Let's listen to Jesus' teachings and then compare them with the theology that came out of the book of Romans.

Matthew

5:38-39: *"You have heard that it was said, 'An eye for an eye, and a tooth for a tooth.' But now I tell you: do not take revenge on someone who wrongs you. If anyone slaps you on the right cheek, let him slap your left cheek too."*

5:40-42: *"If someone takes you to court to sue you for your shirt, let him have your coat as well. And if one of the occupation troops forces you to carry his pack one mile, carry it two miles. When someone asks you for something, give it to him; when someone wants to borrow something, lend it to him."*

5:43-45: *"You have heard that it was said, 'Love your friends, hate your enemies.' But now I tell you: love your enemies and pray for those who persecute you, so that you may become the children of your Father in heaven. For he makes his sun to shine on bad and good people alike, and gives rain to those who do good and to those who do evil."*

6:31-33: *"Do not start worrying: Where will my food come from? or my drink? or my clothes?...Your Father in heaven knows that you need all these things. Instead, be concerned above everything else with the Kingdom of God and with what he requires of you, and he will provide you with all these other things."*

7:12: *"Do for others what you want them to do for you."*

9:13: *"Go and find out what is meant by the scripture that says: It is kindness that I want, not animal sacrifices."*

18:2-4: *"Jesus called a child to come and stand in front of them, and said, 'I assure you that unless you change and become like children, you will never enter the Kingdom of heaven. The greatest in* the Kingdom of heaven is the one who humbles himself and becomes like this child.'"

18:19-20: *"Whenever two of you on earth agree about anything you pray for, it will be done for you by my Father in heaven. For where two or three come together in my name, I am there with them."*

20:26-27: *"If one of you wants to be great, you must be the servant of the rest; and if one of you wants to be first, you must be the slave of the others."*

25:40: *"I tell you, whenever you did this for one of the least important of these followers of mine, you did it for me!"*

John

13:34-35: *"I give you a new commandment: love one another. As I have loved you, so you must love one another. If you have love for one another, then everyone will know that you are my disciples."*

16:12-15: *"I have much more to tell you, but now it would be too much for you to bear. When, however, the Spirit comes, who reveals the truth about God, he will lead you into all the truth."*

By contrast, if you look at the book of Romans, you will discover passages such as this, in chapter 10:9-10: *"If you confess that Jesus is Lord and believe that God raised him from death, you will be saved. For it is by our faith that we are put right with God; it is by our confession that we are saved."*

The focus here and in much of the epistle is on personal righteousness and how to make certain that you will be saved. That focus is inward, selfish. Now, look again at these teachings of Jesus. They are all focused outward toward others. They tell us how to live in peace and love with others in the Kingdom. Jesus doesn't discuss salvation because he knows that we don't need to be saved. We are already one with God. All we have to do is accept that fact and bear the fruits of Kingdom love.

But Paul can't shake his legalistic Jewish heritage. He didn't walk with Jesus, didn't hear him preach, never got a sense of the new Kingdom which he was proclaiming. And so the only thing he knew how to do was to take a step backward into the Law, into a search for righteousness, and dress up the old ideas in newer language. His concern was that we make ourselves acceptable to God. He couldn't believe Jesus' claim that we are already accepted.

Romans 1:18-19: *"God's anger is revealed from heaven against all the sin and evil of the people whose evil ways prevent the truth from being known. God punishes them."* The difference in tone between this and the teachings of Jesus is remarkable.

Romans 2:5: *"You have a hard and stubborn heart, and so you are making your own punishment even greater on the Day when God's anger and righteous judgments will be revealed."* It doesn't sound as though Paul is even talking about the same God that Jesus came to reveal. The righteous and angry God of the Old Testament still overpowers in Paul's mind the new view of God that Jesus is trying to introduce.

Romans 2:13: *"For it is not by hearing the Law that people are put right with God, but by doing what the Law commands."* Paul can't unhook himself from the old Law in which he has been trained, just as many of us find it hard to adopt this new way of looking at God; it means giving up the fear of God which we have been taught since our Sunday School days. It's true that Paul often says that the Law won't save us, but then he merely converts the old Law into a new one – he insists that we are saved only through our faith in Jesus Christ who came to redeem us by his death on the cross. The Old Testament Law said, in effect, obey or die. The new Christian law, in his opinion, says almost the same thing – believe or die.

So, much of the church's belief system is based on Paulinistic thinking. By contrast, the teachings of Jesus are simple and clear. But they are also far too demanding for the average church member. They require self-sacrifice, unselfishness, spiritual openness, profound love for others, and the willingness to give up personal desires for the advancement of the Kingdom on Earth. That's what Jesus wanted us to do as his disciples. But how many people are really willing to love their enemies, to give away their possessions, to turn the other cheek, and to put the Kingdom ahead of everything? It's far easier to obey a few rules and be told that, as a result, we will go to heaven. Most people find it far more desirable to work on their own salvation than to sacrifice in order to make the world a better place. Which means that most "Christians" are disciples of Paul rather than Jesus!

The Bible is not the Word of God because Paul has kidnapped the message of Jesus and stuffed it inside an Old Testament mindset. The real Word of God is found in Jesus' teachings. The idea that Paul's theology is the Good News of the Gospel is one more myth. Paul spent the rest of his life trying to find the key to the Kingdom. But Jesus had come to tell us that the door to the Kingdom has always been unlocked; we don't need a key! We're already inside the gate. Now all we have to do is learn how to live together in the Kingdom. And that will require many lifetimes of struggle, as we discover how to cast off our ego and allow the grace of God to make us one with each other and with the universe.

Chapter Six

Jesus

Jesus Is Not God

In the following chapter, I don't wish to express any disrespect to Jesus of Nazareth. He has been a major part of my youth, my family, and my profession. I have great love and admiration for this towering historical figure who has come to represent love for God and for our fellow human beings. He came to announce the establishment of the Kingdom of God on Earth, and working for the growth of that Kingdom should be the primary occupation for anyone who calls himself Jesus' disciple.

I want to honor Jesus in this chapter, but in a way which will trouble conservatives. I want to remove the burden of divinity from his shoulders so that we can see him as a human being like we are, which will better enable us to become the kind of human being that he was.

Let's begin with the question as to whether Jesus was a real man. This is by no means a certain thing, since his historical existence has always been debated. In I John 4:2-3, we read: *"Anyone who acknowledges that Jesus Christ came as a human being has the Spirit who comes from God. But anyone who denies this about Jesus does not have the Spirit from God. The spirit that he has is from the Enemy of Christ."* So there were people as far back as the time of the New Testament writers who questioned whether the incarnation had really happened. But let's assume that it did. Jesus lived in the first century, and received a commission to teach people that God was in their midst. He was disturbed by the religious climate of his day which was so focused on personal righteousness that the needs of the poor went unmet. He sensed that religion had become a moneymaking business filled with meaningless routine; it was dominated by a burdensome set of laws which had nothing to do with spirituality and everything to do with ego and pride. He came to change that system into one in which people would be willing to love God and their neighbor, and to live in peace and mutual cooperation as a sign that the Kingdom was in their midst. In other words, he came to get rid of religion and establish true spirituality.

He may well have been able to heal, since he seems to have known the connection between mind and body. We know he was a spellbinding teacher and that his stories were collected and shared among his followers. He may also have possessed certain skills which allowed him to do things that the people of his time could only view as miracles.

Beyond that, we run into a wall. He was not God in human form, he did not have the power to walk on water or move mountains. He did not bring dead people back to life, turn water into wine or walk out of his tomb in a resurrected physical body. God has designed us so that these things are impossible for human beings. Yet, we have been taught that these things proved that Jesus was God in human flesh. But the Bible is not recounting actual history when it tells these stories. And therefore we must conclude that these things can happen only in…myths.

Why do we think that God must become a human being before we as human beings can fully interact with Him? We already have a spirit which is part of His spirit. That is connection enough; it is more direct and personal than having to relate to God through another human being, even one as advanced as Jesus. The irony is this: Jesus is physically gone from the Earth, so the only way we can relate to him is spiritually. Thus, Jesus is merely a symbol for God, and he came to tell us that we no longer need an intercessor. We have direct access to God. The Kingdom is in our midst.

The disciples were convinced that Jesus had come to change the world, to create a new divine Kingdom on Earth. And they were right. But they didn't believe that a mere human being had the power to do these things. They were convinced that such ability could come only from a god. And so, after his death, as they thought about what Jesus had done, they saw him as more and more godlike. And they were so devastated by his bureaucratic murder that they had to assign some cosmic plan to his life and death, in order to make sense of it all. And to do so, they did what countless religions before them had done – they created a myth. They not only invented their own story about the life and ministry of this god-man, they also borrowed from other religious myths to enhance the profile of this teacher whom they idolized.

The "dying god myth" is common to many ancient religions. It tells of a god who is born, is put to death, passes through a phase in the underworld among the dead, and is subsequently reborn, in either a literal or symbolic sense.

Krishna, a Hindu deity who was worshipped as a god thousands of years before Jesus' birth, is claimed to have said and done many of the things attributed later to Jesus – he had a miraculous birth, taught about salvation and worked miracles, was considered the savior of men, was killed by being suspended on a tree, was raised from the dead and ascended to heaven.

The same miraculous claims are made for Mithra, whose roots go back to Zoroastrianism, a Persian religion popular in Greece fifteen centuries before the coming of Jesus. It is said that Mithra was born of a virgin, that he had twelve followers or disciples, that he performed miracles, was killed and resurrected, and that he was known as mankind's savior and was called the light of the world. His followers worshipped him on Sunday and celebrated a Eucharist together. The religion's priests were called magi, and they had predicted the coming of a Messiah, which is why magi came from the east to see if Jesus was that Messiah. Mithraism had its beginning in Tarsus, Paul's hometown, and it's likely that Paul mixed his knowledge of Mithraism with his understanding of the Jewish longing for the Messiah, and came up with his version of the Jesus religion.

There's an interesting note concerning crucifixion in a book by Thomas Doane.[9] He quotes one of the Church Fathers as late as AD

211 who said that, while Christians did not worship crosses, pagans did, and not just a cross but one with a man on it. It apparently represented a savior who was crucified for the salvation of mankind; this was long before the Christian era. These "crucifixes" were said to have been found in many places all over Italy. The practice of sacrificing human beings for the atonement of sin was common in ancient Egypt. In India, in pre-Christian times, the idea of redemption by the divine incarnation of a god, who came into the world for the express purpose of saving mankind, was a general and popular belief.

Now, let's review some revealing information that puts the whole question of Jesus in an entirely different light.[10] There is good reason to believe that the Christian myth is partly based on the ancient astrological traditions of pagan religions. Sun worship was almost universal among these early societies, including the Roman Empire, and the sun was the most popular god in the heathen pantheon. Without the sun, nothing will grow, and life would be impossible. In addition, the sun conquers the darkness of night with all of its threats and terrors. The birth, death, and resurrection of the sun was a daily story with a variety of sun gods: Adonis, Bacchus, Hercules, Khrishna, Mithra, and Osiris.

In these early religions, the sun became the symbol of the invisible creator of the universe, and was variously called the son of God, the light of the world, the savior of mankind. It's interesting to note that our traditional time of worship is still called Sun-day. Roman Catholic and many other church buildings face east, the direction of the rising sun, so that early Christians were thought at first to be sun-worshippers.

December 21 is the winter solstice. The word "solstice" comes from the Latin words *sol* and *sistere*, meaning "sun" and "standing still." On this date, the sun reaches its extreme southern point, and in the northern hemisphere this produces the shortest day of the year. Then the sun appears to remain unmoving for three days, after which it begins its slow movement north once again.

This midwinter day was a significant moment in early religious mythology. On the 21st of December, the sun appears to die – that is, to stop its normal movement south. Some have pointed out that it dies in the vicinity of the Southern Cross which can be seen from the north only during this time of the year. So the sun dies, appearing to hang on a cross, remains dead for three days, and comes back to life – is reborn – on December 25. The Romans had a huge celebration on this day, called The Birthday of the Unconquered Sun.

It doesn't take much imagination to see how the early Christians, in order to win over their pagan neighbors who still worshipped the sun, merely incorporated those beliefs into their Jesus story. Sun (Son?) died on a cross, remained dead for three days, and rose on the third day to bring new life to the Earth. That is the Easter story, but it was not celebrated until the spring equinox because that is the time when the sun finally conquers the darkness, and the days become longer than the nights. In the meantime, the rebirth of the sun on December 25 was transformed into the birth of the Son in the developing Christian religion. So the two major festivals of the Christian year – Christmas and Easter – are both positioned on the calendar on the basis of the movement of the sun – the winter solstice and the spring equinox – a clear connection to early pagan practices.

Other astrological details concerning Jesus' birth include the star of Bethlehem. Assuming that it was Sirius, the brightest star in the night sky, it lines up with the three stars in what we know as Orion's belt. These stars were called The Three Kings. Together with Sirius, they point to the place where the sun will rise on December 25. So it can be said that the three kings follow the star moving toward the sunrise, the place where the sun is going to be born.

Easter, as we have indicated, is based on astrological movements. The name Easter means "east," toward the rising sun. The festival is called a "moveable feast" because it can fall anywhere between March 22 and April 25. Its date is determined by the position of the sun and the phases of the moon. It is the Sun-day after the first full moon following the spring equinox, the day when the sun finally triumphs over darkness. The Son's triumph over the darkness of sin and death takes place just when we have hope for the warmer, brighter days of the spring season. It's interesting to remember, incidentally, that one of the features of the death of Jesus is that darkness came over the land for three hours, symbolizing the death of God's Sun.

The stars were also important to the early pagans, who thought of them as gods who possessed powers which controlled their lives. They organized the stars into a complex series of constellations, personalizing them as humans and animals. There were twelve of them which divided the year into months; when they were arranged into a zodiacal chart, with the sun at the center, they represented the twelve months, the four seasons, and the two solstices and equinoxes.

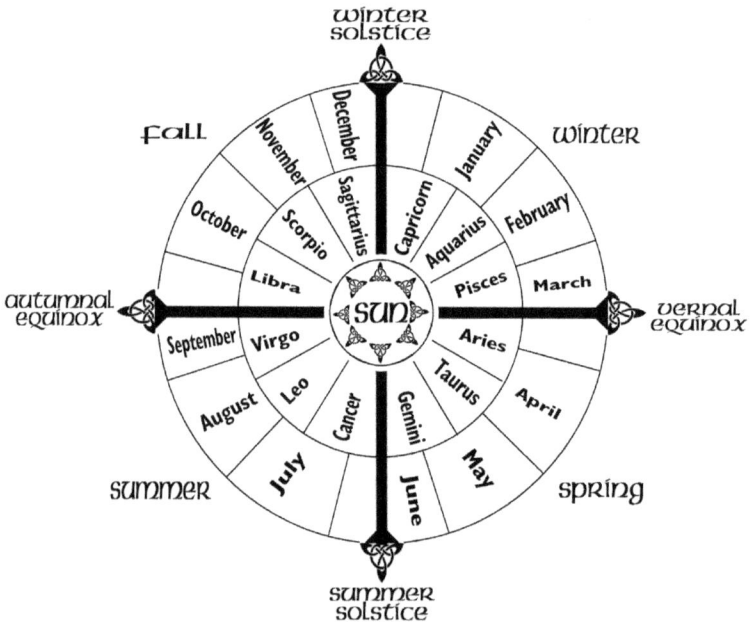

The sun travels through the group of twelve starry companions throughout the year, just as Jesus, the Son, travelled with his twelve companions. The constant appearance in scripture of the number twelve is not a coincidence; it is a clear astrological reference.

The Celtic cross, common to Ireland, Wales and Scotland, is in fact a shorthand image for the zodiacal chart, with the circle at the center representing the sun, and the cross bars being the equinox and solstice dividers. This symbol is believed to have its origin in Druid sun worship.

Jesus is often represented with those three cross bars radiating from the sides and the top of his head; his head is at the center of the cross in the place of the sun. This symbolism makes him the sun of God, the light of the world, with the rays of the sun shining in a halo about his head. His promise to come again is a reference to the ancient hope that the sun will rise again each morning to counteract the works of darkness.

Jesus lived in the astrological age of Pisces, the two fish. He calls as his first disciples two fishermen; he feeds the 5000 with bread and two fish; he calls his disciples to become fishers of men; some Christians have been commanded to eat fish as part of their spiritual observance; and even today the symbol of Christ is a fish.

The word for "fish" in Greek is "Ichthus," spelled in the Greek language by the five letters above. But they can also be used as the initial letters of the phrase, "Jesus Christ, God's Son, Savior." This is why it was easy for the early Christians to adopt the Pisces symbol as their identifying sign.

So, much of what we know as Christian tradition and practice can be shown to have roots in astrological philosophy. Many believers reject claims that Christianity is an amalgam of ideas from previous religious traditions. But it is clear that no religion starts from scratch. Most religions have the same general agenda – love of God, love for our fellow humans, and hope for eternal life in paradise. But since God is so far away and seemingly unreachable, we need to invent beings who represent God, like the little boy who wanted a god with skin on his face.

So do we all, and that is why we come up with stories about gods who come down from their exalted thrones and put on our human flesh so that they can tell their people how much they love them.

Other famous gods who were also born on December 25 include Krishna of India, 3228 BC; Horus of Egypt, 2500 BC; Mithra of Persia, c. 1500 BC; and Buddha of India, 563 BC. This is not merely some divine coincidence. When we understand the astrological significance of that date, it becomes clear that these various stories all have the same theme – God came to Earth, brought light into the darkness, suffered to redeem humankind, and rose to new life to ensure that believers would live forever. The message is the same, regardless of differences in culture, historical era, or religion. Seen in this light, it becomes very difficult to believe that the details of the Jesus story are anything other than myth.

Jesus is not God. But I will agree with those who say that he was a son of God. Not the son of God, but a son of God just like the rest of us, since we are all sons and daughters of God. Jesus made it clear that he identified with us when he called himself the Son of Man rather than the Son of God. What do we make of his promise that we will do greater things than he did? Either we have the potential to do greater things than God can do, or Jesus is a human being who is still evolving, and who expects us to evolve even beyond what he has already achieved.

If Jesus was God, we could not have identified with him. He would have been a totally different class of being. But because he was human, he is the kind of person with whom we could sit down and have a cup of coffee and chat about the ballgame as well as the state of the Kingdom. We think of him as too holy to be human, and that keeps him at arm's length. But he enjoyed himself with common earthly pleasures and the fellowship of others, just like we do, so much so that some people called him a drunk. In Luke 7:34, he says, *"The Son of Man came, and he ate and drank, and you said, 'Look at this man! He is a glutton and wine drinker, a friend of tax collectors and other outcasts!'"*

So, he was one of us. But he was also a spiritual master. That is the true purpose of a person like Jesus, to tell us in compelling ways, "I am like you. And what I have done, you can do too because we are both children of God."

Chapter Seven

Theology

The 20th century saw the rise of fundamentalism, an effort to counteract the increasing influence of modernist theology. The term "fundamentalism" was taken from the title of a series of essays published from 1910-1915 by the Bible Institute of Los Angeles, *The Fundamentals: A Testimony to the Truth.*

The leaders of this movement included the Baptists and Presbyterians among others, many of them from a Calvinist background. These groups subscribed to a set of beliefs which they called the Five Fundamentals, and they claimed that refusal to believe any one of the five marked the person as a non-Christian. These five basic beliefs included:

> *The inerrancy of the Bible*
> *The virgin birth of Jesus Christ*
> *The doctrine of substitutionary atonement*
> *The bodily resurrection of Jesus*
> *The imminent personal return of Jesus Christ.*

Let's discuss these fundamental beliefs of the Christian faith, and see how they hold up in the light of reason, common sense and science.

1. The inerrancy of the Bible

I believe we've dealt with this sufficiently in chapter five. Let's remember that the Bible was written by men who, while they felt themselves inspired by God, were still subject to human error and to the ideas that were current at their moment in history. The very first chapter of the Bible illustrates that the Bible is *not* inerrant: it reports that the universe was created in six days. When people try to make the first chapter of Genesis a factual description of creation, in order to maintain the fiction that every word in the Bible is literally true, they merely appear foolish and uneducated. Archbishop James Ussher of Ireland, some 400 years ago, using biblical references, calculated that the first day of creation began in the evening preceding Sunday, October 23, 4004 BC. What's more surprising is that many people accept that as fact! The idea of biblical inerrancy makes us believe and say some peculiar things.

One of those peculiar things has to do with women: Is the Bible inerrant when it says that women should be subservient to men in the church? The fact that we are still fighting that kind of religious bigotry is witness to how destructive it can be to think of scripture as inerrant and authoritative for today's world.

When we claim that the Bible is the final and complete Word of God, it creates a situation in which we can quit listening to what God has to say to us today. Make no mistake, God is still revealing His truth to us at this moment in time, just as in the period of the scriptural authors. But if we are convinced that we already have all of God's truth written down in a book, accurate to the last comma and crossed t, there's no use in looking for anything more. And this is a problem because Jesus, as we have said repeatedly, has promised that he has much more to tell us.

It comes down to a matter of control. When we have the final inerrant word of God in our church, *we* are in control. We can make judgments about people and ideas and events based on what has been revealed in the past through the words in this book.

But when we understand that God is still delivering His revelations to us, through modern prophets who are able to hear the voice of the Holy Spirit, then we are faced with the fact that it is *God* who is in control. And conservatives are especially afraid of this situation. It upsets the neat little systems they have created and which they proclaim to be the final truth. When God provides us with new information, it changes our understanding of who God is, and this confuses us. The new insights demand that we change and grow; but orthodoxy can't stand change because it requires that we rethink our ancient ideas about God.

The truth is, we have invented the god whom the church worships; we have created God in our own image. So when God speaks to us with updated information concerning what the divine world is all about, it disagrees with our childish models. As a result, it presents us with the choice between our own traditions, which are comforting, and the truth of God, which is fresh and startling. With that choice before us, which one do we choose? It's not surprising to learn that most conservative people choose the former. Tradition is a lot safer than being open to the presence and power of God. But it's the difference between worshipping a book and worshipping the divine presence.

Those who act the most religious are often the ones who are most afraid of God. Ironic, isn't it? They are afraid that if they break the rules, God will judge them, which is why they are so scrupulous about obeying all the rules. They are afraid that if they open up to the Spirit, God will make them think, and change, and do things they don't want to do. They can't decide whether openness pleases God or angers Him. So they would rather remain within their religious myths than venture into the world of spirit, ready to hear what God has to say. By choosing safety and intellectual comfort, they turn their backs on God, and in the process miss the greatest spiritual adventure of all.

2. The virgin birth of Jesus

The next doctrine which is a required belief by the conservative wing of the church is the Virgin Birth. Such a thing is biologically impossible, a contradiction of God's own laws of nature. But we need to be aware that some form of miraculous birth has traditionally accompanied many of the god/men who were worshipped in various ancient religions.

Krishna, for instance, was born of a "chaste virgin" named Devaki who was selected to become the "mother of God." Gautama Buddha was born of the Virgin Maya or Mary. The Siamese believed in a virgin-born god and savior whom they called Codom. While in prayer, his mother was impregnated by sunbeams. China had a similar mythology. One of the religions of China believed in a virgin-born god/man named Fo-hi who was born in 3468 BC. When his mother conceived him miraculously, witnesses saw her surrounded by a rainbow. The first Jesuit missionaries to China were shocked when they found that people believed in a god whose birth was so similar to that of Jesus.

This is a clear example of how classic mythic stories eventually became attributed to Jesus. That was done to underline the divinity of the prophet, to show that God held him in special favor, and to demonstrate that he had special powers which would bless those who worshipped him. But we, as modern objective believers, can clearly see this as one more myth which has always been part of the larger Christian mythology.

The problem with demanding that believers accept miraculous religious events as fact is that it puts religious dogma outside the realm of human reality and experience. If we believe in a god who comes to Earth by means of breaking the rules which bind us as humans, and who continues to break the laws of nature by performing works which are impossible for us, we can be nothing but observers of these awe-inspiring events.

But this should not be the function of religion, to produce awe and nothing more. The contemplation of God is sufficiently awe-inspiring without requiring Him to break His own laws in order to impress us. Rather, religion should do just the opposite. Jesus' promise about our potential to do even greater things than he did makes this clear. The basic reason for the incarnation was to bring the knowledge of God down to our level, *so that we could be inspired to transcend to His level.* God is saying in Jesus, not that we are helpless in the presence of God, not that we are powerless sinners who need to be saved from our own fallen nature, but that we are like Jesus and can eventually share in the freedom and power that Jesus came to demonstrate.

3. The doctrine of substitutionary atonement

This whole concept is based on primitive ideas about how the gods were to be propitiated. It began with human sacrifice: a young maiden, for instance, would be thrown into a volcano to keep the god of the volcano from erupting and destroying their village. Remnants of this pre-Jewish practice can be seen in the story in Genesis 22 where Abraham is willing to sacrifice his only son, Isaac, in order to please God.

But the Bible itself argues against this practice. In the book of Micah, chapter 6, the question is asked, *"Shall I offer him my first-born child to pay for my sins?"* And the response comes in these words: *"No, the Lord has told us what is good. What he requires of us is this: to do what is just, to show constant love, and to live in humble fellowship with our God."*

In Jeremiah 7:30-31, God is even more specific about the horrible practice of human sacrifice. *"The people of Judah have done an evil thing...They have built an altar...so that they can sacrifice their sons and daughters in the fire. I did not command them to do this – it did not even enter my mind."*

To the Jews, life was in the blood – spill a person's blood, and that person dies. So blood is a symbol of the life of the individual. When a person sins, according to the Jews, God is justified in punishing that person with death. In other words, his blood (life) is forfeit to God. But when human sacrifice was no longer practiced, where was the blood to be acquired which would persuade God to forgive sins? In Hebrews 9:22 it says that *"sins are forgiven only if blood is poured out."* That idea was so deeply embedded in the Hebrew mind that a substitute for human blood had to be found.

The most obvious solution was for a man to purchase an animal which could be sacrificed in his place. Then the spilling of the animal's blood would be considered by God to be the spilling of the man's blood, so that righteousness could prevail and the man's sins be forgiven.

Later, when the early Christian theologians were looking for a way to describe God's forgiveness, this tradition was already in place and could easily be adapted to express God's relationship to us through Jesus. The lamb was one of the main animals used in the Temple's sacrificial rites, so it was natural to view Jesus as the sacrificial lamb – the lamb of God that takes away the sins of the world – a substitute sacrifice which we could use to be forgiven and escape punishment. The Old Testament connection is clear here: Abraham was ready to sacrifice his only son, and now God is also ready to sacrifice His only son.

The theory works this way: We are all sinners; we all deserve to die to satisfy God's justice. Jesus is a man like us, but without sin. So he doesn't deserve to die because he is perfect. But he dies anyway, killed on the cross by religious people. Since he didn't owe his death to God, there is now a treasury of merit – Jesus' blood innocently spilled – waiting to be used by others who seek God's forgiveness. The Christian tradition is filled with images of being washed in that blood, of a fountain filled with blood drawn from Immanuel's veins which could purify even the most evil sinner.

Fundamentalists, who insist on this belief, take literally the statement that there is no remission of sin without the spilling of blood. But this is nothing less than the adoption of ancient pagan practices, another example of how beliefs from other even more primitive religions were tacked onto Christianity.

In the Micah passage already cited, God makes it clear that it is not blood sacrifice which is desired, but justice, mercy and humility before God. In Hosea 6:6, God says essentially the same thing: *"I want your constant love, not your animal sacrifices. I would rather have my people know me than burn offerings to me."*

Think about it this way. The common way to access the forgiving blood of Jesus is to make a public profession of faith. You are encouraged to "plead the blood," to ask God in Jesus' name to forgive your sins and accept you as a redeemed sinner, saved by grace. Then what happens? You are considered "converted" and are called to live a life of love and service.

But you are the same person after that ritual. Was the blood really necessary or was it merely a metaphor? God accepts us, post-conversion, not because we visualized being washed in 2000 year-old blood but because we have always belonged to God, and God will not reject His own. The "conversion" we have undergone has nothing to do with a blood bath (interesting term!). Nothing has changed except our perspective; we have moved from a selfish earthly viewpoint to one which sees God in our lives in every moment of the day.

It is time to move away from the ugly echoes of those horrible pagan practices, and to understand that the Kingdom has to do with love and peace, not blood. We do not need some complicated ritual to come into God's presence. All we need are eyes to see what has always been there, an open door and a world filled with light.

4. The bodily resurrection of Jesus

Religions are filled with miraculous events and yet, while I do not deny the existence of the miraculous, the clustering of extraordinary claims for the Jesus story makes it clear that those who developed the faith packed it with enough supernatural detail to push the limits of credibility today.

The central event of the Christian faith is the resurrection. Did it happen, or did it not? The debate on this one issue has lasted for 2,000 years because it is the linchpin of the entire faith system. Without it, the fundamental promise of the Gospel – that we as believers will be raised from death just as Jesus was – is deflated and loses its authority.

The conflict here is between those who claim merely that Jesus was alive in some form after Easter, and those who hold that Jesus' dead body was reanimated and subsequently ascended into heaven. This latter claim requires us to believe that Jesus' physical body was taken up into a spiritual heaven. Any objective consideration of this view will conclude that it is impossible. The idea of a physically resurrected body entering heaven is not a miracle, it is an absurdity.

In the first place, heaven is not a physical place. The ancient Jews had a poorly developed understanding of the hereafter and may well have thought that a physical body could exist there. But in our day, we have a more evolved view of the difference between the spiritual and physical worlds. We know that they are two entirely different states of being. When we die, our *spirit* enters that other world, not our physical body. To insist that a physical body can exist in heaven is similar to thinking that we can walk through a television screen and greet the people in the movie we are watching. Both ideas are impossible.

So, what does that leave us with? First of all, Mark, the earliest of the gospel writers, did not include anything about Jesus' resurrection in the initial version of his book. He ended the story with an empty tomb and the disciples "distressed and terrified." The account of the resurrection in current versions of Mark's gospel was apparently added at a later time, to make it correspond with the other three gospels. So we have to consider that there may have been no resurrection at all, based on this earliest documentary evidence.

Let's say that there *was* an empty tomb. What happened to Jesus? One answer is that he appeared to the disciples in his spirit form. This is an answer which is acceptable today. Our website, www.beyondreligion.com, contains dozens of stories about After Death Communications (ADC's), appearances to their loved ones by deceased persons. Many people no longer question the validity of this phenomenon, which leaves open the possibility that this might have been the form in which Jesus appeared to his disciples.

But since the Jews had no real understanding of the spirit world, and tended to think in concrete terms, it is not surprising that they concluded that the post-resurrection Jesus was a physical being. Luke – or perhaps his later redactors – even adds a note in 24:39 in which Jesus insists that he is not a ghost. But it is easy to see that this is merely an attempt to prove that the resurrection really happened. And, in any event, it throws us right back into the issue of a physical body ascending to a spiritual heaven.

So, what did happen to Jesus' body, if it was his spirit which appeared to his disciples? Matthew 28 contains a verse suggesting that the guards had been bribed: they said that the disciples stole his body in order to tell everyone that he had come back to life. This is another possibility. If the story actually ended where the gospel of Mark suggests it did, with Jesus dead, his followers might simply have reburied him elsewhere, and let the myth about his rising from the dead develop over time.

Then there is the Shroud of Turin. I must admit my fascination with this unique artifact. Because it is a photographic negative which has 3-D information coded within it, it is something more than a common burial wrapping. There are those who see it as proof of the resurrection. John 20 tells us that Peter was the first one into the tomb, and that he saw *"the linen cloths lying there, and the cloth which had been around Jesus' head. It was not lying with the linen cloths but was rolled up by itself."*

This might well have been the Shroud, except for one problem. Note that the record says "cloths," plural. The Shroud is singular. The passage also makes the point that there was an additional cloth, the one that had been around his head. This is apparently the Sudarium which is now kept in the Cathedral of San Salvador in Oviedo, Spain. It was a smaller cloth which was put over the face of Jesus after he died, out of respect for his family's sensibilities. It has the same type of blood as that on the Shroud, AB, and, although there is no image on the cloth, the arrangement of the markings exactly matches those of the facial image on the Shroud.

The question arises: if the cloth was on Jesus' face when he was buried in the Shroud, why is his facial image not on the Sudarium instead of on the Shroud? But the passage in John makes clear that it was rolled up by itself, which may suggest that it was removed before the Shroud was put in place. In any event, the Shroud, or "cloths," were lying where Jesus' body had been, but the body was gone. What happened to it?

Scientists, who have carefully examined the Shroud on several occasions in recent years, using the latest and most sophisticated equipment, are at a loss to explain how the image was imprinted on the material. Believers, on the other hand, explain it readily by saying that at the moment of the resurrection, there must have been a burst of radiation or some other sort of energy, and this energy burned the image into the very tips of the shroud's fibers. But this belief is in support of the idea that his body came to life again. If that was the case, the Shroud would have had to be unwrapped from around him in order to free his body. Is it likely that it would then have been rearranged in the same position on the stone slab which it had occupied before the resurrection, as the Bible account seems to suggest?

There is another theory which may answer some of these questions but which provides a new set of mysteries. What if there *was* a burst of energy which imprinted the image, but the energy was for the purpose of *dematerializing* the body? Is this idea any more remarkable than the thought of the body coming back to life? It would account for the image on the cloth, and it would solve the problem of having to deal with a reanimated physical body. But do things like this really happen, or is this just one more mythological attempt to explain the unexplainable?

So we are left with our question only partly answered. First, what we refer to as the resurrection did not produce a resuscitated physical body. Dead people do not rise to life after three days, not even Jesus. The Bible makes this clear when it describes Jesus' post-resurrection appearances. It says that he was unrecognizable to some of his closest friends, and that he could appear and disappear at will. He may well have appeared in his spirit form to his disciples, a form which they wrongly understood to be flesh and blood. Otherwise, the account is so filled with confusion and doubt that it appears to be the product of the myth which grew up around him.

But when we dwell on this mystery too long, we miss the whole point of Easter. That point is that Jesus was *alive* after his physical death. It didn't take a resurrection for this to be true. He was alive because he is part of God and God is alive eternally. And the message to us is that because he lives, we too will live, not because Jesus died for us, not because we follow a religion which teaches that a man once walked out of his own tomb, but because we are like Jesus, created in God's image, part of eternity. This is the really good news, and the underlying message of Easter morning.

5. The imminent personal return of Jesus Christ

This is the other side of the idea that Jesus entered heaven in his physical body. Many believe that he will return in his physical body, to collect those who believe in him and to set in motion the end of the world. I've often thought that if Jesus did return and start talking about God, the conservatives who seem most enthusiastic about the Second Coming might well be first in line to nail him to a cross again for heresy, just as they did the first time.

A Baptist preacher named William Miller predicted that Jesus would return on October 22, 1844. He attracted many thousands of people around the world to what eventually became a cult called Millerism. Many of his followers quit their jobs and got rid of their possessions as the date neared. On October 22, they put on their white ascension robes, and many of them stood on their rooftops to be as near the descending Jesus as possible. But of course nothing happened. That whole fiasco is known as "The Great Disappointment." But that kind of nonsense isn't limited to the 1800's. A radio preacher named Harold Camping predicted that the Second Coming would happen on May 21, 2011. He collected quite a few followers but, again, it was another great disappointment.

From looking at the state of the world today, you can draw two conclusions: either it is so corrupt and sinful that God is going to punish it with destruction sometime soon; or, its corruption and sinfulness are evidence that we are in the infancy of our evolvement, and we have a very long way still to go. God didn't create the universe in order to blow us to bits when He got a little peeved at our behavior. Remember what the rainbow promised after Noah's ark landed? God said He would never again destroy His people. OK, so that's a myth too, but you get the idea.

It has taken billions of years to get us to this point. God is not going to stop things for religious reasons any time soon. The world will probably not end until the earth gets sucked into the sun in about 7.6 billion years. Of course, that's another prediction which may be about as reliable as the one in 2011. But, in any event, we probably shouldn't waste any time sitting expectantly on our roof.

Chapter Eight

The Church

The Church Is More Political Than Spiritual.

In addition to ruling the Roman Catholic masses, the popes also ruled an area known as the Papal States for over 1000 years. This meant that they were as involved as the kings of other nations in geopolitical and military disputes, coalitions, and negotiations. The popes, representatives of the Prince of Peace, waged war, signed treaties, and involved themselves in all the political intrigues of that period.

On Nov. 27, 1095, Pope Urban II authorized a crusade to liberate Jerusalem by force of arms from the Muslims who had conquered it. This was the First Crusade and is an instance when the leader of the Christian church called his people to engage in a war against the church's enemies.

The Crusaders considered Jews, whom they called "Christ-killers," to be enemies of God. They gave the Jews whom they encountered two choices – become Christians or die. In the Rhine Valley alone, 12,000 Jews were killed by the soldiers of the first Crusade. Some Jewish writers refer to this event as "the first holocaust."

Pope Paul III began the Roman Inquisition in 1542. It is estimated that out of the thousands of people judged by the Inquisition in Italy, around 1,250 were executed. This mass murder was so successful that by the end of the 16th century, almost all traces of Protestantism had been wiped out in Italy.

Mary I of England was a Roman Catholic at a time when England was struggling to break free of Rome and become Protestant. Mary, upon her accession in 1553, made it clear that she would do everything in her power as queen to keep England Catholic. She had nearly 300 people burned at the stake for heresy, including the former Archbishop of Canterbury, Thomas Cranmer. This monstrous activity earned her the nickname "Bloody Mary."

In 1616, Pope Gregory XV convened a group of canon law scholars who reported that the sun is not stationary, that it is not at the center of the solar system, and that the Earth does not move around the sun. In their judgment, anyone who believed that these ideas were true was a heretic. This group tried Galileo in 1633, condemning him for a "grave suspicion of heresy," and banned all his works. He was still under house arrest when he died in 1642. The Catholic church couldn't see its way clear to correct this egregious mistake for over 350 years. Technically, Roman Catholics didn't believe that the sun was the center of the solar system until 1992!

Both sides, Catholic and Protestant, have been equally guilty of horrifying actions in the name of God. In 1792, French revolutionaries in Paris, believing that the Roman Catholic church did not support their goals, attacked and killed many priests at a Carmelite convent. Other priests had been imprisoned there by the government for refusing to take an oath of loyalty to the French Revolution. By the time the killing was over, the toll would include two hundred priests and three bishops. Many of those who lost their lives would be beatified in 1926.

In the mid 1980's, the world was shocked when Roman Catholic sex abuse cases began to come to light. The worst part of the scandal was the revelation that the Catholic hierarchy had tried to keep the scandal a secret. Instead of dealing with the situation openly and honestly, the bishops frequently reassigned the offenders to other parishes so that these sexual-predator priests could continue to abuse children. The church has paid more than two billion dollars in compensation to the various victims.

In Ireland, a study called the Ryan Report, published in May 2009, revealed that nuns and priests had been responsible for the beatings and humiliation of up to 30,000 children over many decades at institutions owned by the church, while government inspectors failed to stop the abuse. The story was dramatized in 2002 in a film entitled *The Magdalene Sisters.*

The above list of abuses runs from 1095 to the modern day, an entire millennium filled with outrages committed in the name of Jesus Christ. Is it any wonder that outsiders, reading about the church's history, express doubts about its integrity as a religious institution?

I'm not singling out the Roman Catholic church. It's just that they have been in business longer. But I have been a member of the Protestant church long enough to know that grievous sins have been committed on both sides of the church aisle. Whenever either has been in control, each has used questionable methods to spread their particular faith. Our connection to God should be personal, but the church has often made it political, even using force to compel people to accept its religious practices. Conversion at the point of a sword is not what Jesus had in mind when he sent the disciples out to spread the good news of the Gospel to all nations.

I am aware that large portions of the church are doing admirable work, but the fact remains that for most people membership is traditional, habitual, and not very life-altering, and that there is often little difference between the average pew sitter and the person outside on the street who never darkens the church door. One of the classic pop-culture examples of this is Michael Corleone in *The Godfather*, who takes vows in the church promising to renounce the devil and his works while his henchmen are busy murdering his enemies.

When Constantine had his vision of Christ in AD 312 and a year later issued the Edict of Milan, legalizing Christian worship, it seemed like a good thing for the followers of Christ who, up until that time, had been subjected to terrible persecution. But in many ways it was a fatal blow to the idea that the church was called to be the Kingdom of God on Earth. When people risked their lives to attend worship, their faith had to be real and personal. Only those who were sincere about their devotion to Christ could remain faithful in the face of punishment and death.

But as soon as the religion became legal, faith became cheap. It cost nothing to call oneself a Christian. Moreover, many of those in control demanded that their people become Christian for political reasons, and held mass baptisms to enlarge the church rolls. Thus, many were "converted" not for personal spiritual reasons, but out of fear of retribution.

The church gradually moved from spiritual to political concerns, since it was accumulating a larger and larger body of constituents. It spoke for great masses of people, began to accumulate wealth, land and power, and got to the point where it could influence the actions of kings. From then on, it saw itself as a political entity on a par with the kingdoms of this world, to the point where some popes maintained their own armies. That sort of earthly activity, rather than the truths of the Kingdom of Heaven, became the church's overriding concern.

The pope's claim to speak in the name of God gave him added authority which other princes did not share, and so his power to control people became almost absolute. The church's "God-given" weapon of excommunication was used against those who disobeyed its commands, in effect sending them to hell, and the fear of that threat cowed most people and institutions into submission.

When the church reached this point, it felt itself free to do whatever it thought necessary to defend its position and maintain its power. Thus even murder became permissible, rationalized by Old Testament texts in which God instructed His people to slaughter His enemies. All of this happened under the banner of the cross of Christ, despite Jesus' clear message about loving enemies and treating others as we would want to be treated. The incredible perversion and corruption of the church throughout history has been a renunciation of everything it purports to stand for.

It's clear that the church, whose original purpose was to teach its people to follow the example of Jesus, had sold its soul to the world. It was not only in the world, it had resigned its commission and become part of the world. Its social and political dimensions were more important than its desire to teach true spirituality to its members. Its mission had degenerated into an empty set of rituals – attendance at worship, observance of the sacraments, supporting the church financially, and obedience to the dictates of the leadership. The church promised that if people followed these routines, they were guaranteed to get into heaven. Obedience on the part of the people meant power for the hierarchy. It mattered little whether or not the hearts of the masses were truly changed into Christ-likeness.

Throughout its long history, the church needed to preserve its identity. This meant maintaining its traditions, and that in turn required a resistance to change. It has tried to dictate to its people what is true and what is false, and has held on to its historic positions despite clear evidence that some of its views were wrong. Because of this, it is guilty of a kind of anti-intellectualism, trying to enforce beliefs which are manifestly untrue.

The church's battle with Galileo is a prime example. The church, attempting to keep its traditions from changing, tried also to prevent changes in its teaching about the natural world. It had developed a cosmology that fit neatly into its religious worldview, and it was determined to defend that position, even when faced with evidence that its position was wrong. So it turned away from God's truth and demanded that its people accept the church's distorted myth.

The church's attitude with regard to women is another example. Because the Bible was written in a time when women were considered to be the property of men, because the church was founded and led exclusively by men, and because of a continuing prejudice toward the capabilities of women, the church in many cases still denies them their equal rights, and continues to claim that its bigotry in this matter is pleasing to God.

Church politics have resulted in the so-called Body of Christ being split into thousands of fragments. We are not so much interested in *the* truth as we are in *our* truth. When we disagree, we do not look for ways to live together in Christian love and harmony. We pick up our marbles, leave the church and form our own new organization. Many Christians are not on speaking terms with one another, and some are willing to tell other Christians that they are doomed to hell because they belong to the wrong denomination. Our confessions of faith, far from being inspired by the Holy Spirit, are more often products of our rational thinking; they are belief systems which attempt to reduce God to a level which our limited human minds can understand.

And so the church has degenerated in many ways into a religious club that is more akin to the Kiwanis than the Kingdom. It operates by its own humanly-devised set of rules, and it keeps its people in line by applying those rules forcefully. Guilt and fear are still effective tools which the hierarchy uses to manipulate its people.

The Roman Catholic church has long held the principle that "if you give us a child for his first seven years, we will have him for life." I have Catholic friends who will readily admit that they are motivated more by fear and guilt than by any real desire to go to church. Fulfilling religious duties has become a tradition that no one questions any longer, once they have been properly conditioned.

Some of those friends were grateful when their priest began holding mass at 5:00 on Saturday afternoon. Since missing Sunday mass is a sin, attendance at this earlier mass fulfilled their obligation. It also freed them to do more "important" things on Sunday.

This made it clear that they were going to church out of guilt and obligation, not out of the joy of being able to worship God. By trying to sneak out of Sunday worship because they had more important things to do, they were demonstrating that they had no awareness of why Sunday is a holy day. Sunday worship was chosen because it is a celebration of the resurrection of Jesus, a reminder of the central truth of the faith. But they had no sense of that. All they knew was that they were obligated to get their bodies into the church for a mass, and that Saturday at 5:00 caused them the least inconvenience. They were accustomed to giving God the very minimum in this respect. This is what happens when religious practices are mandated, especially when they are backed up by the threat of divine punishment. We have gotten so far away from the grace and freedom of the Gospel that it feels like a return to the burdensome Law of the Old Testament.

The church's refusal to ordain women is in the same category with its unwillingness to approve contraception. The regulation against birth control comes from a time when the church needed as many members as it could get so as to increase its political power base. This goal must be reconsidered in a day when the Earth is overpopulated and myriads of unwanted babies are being born.

The Roman Catholic church contends that preventing pregnancy is on a par with killing children. It maintains, as one of my seminary professors used to explain, that sex is for the purpose of having children, and that the pleasure is simply a bonus. Whereas, according to that professor, the Protestant point of view is just the opposite: the main purpose of sex is the pleasure it gives to married couples, while the baby is the bonus. Those who want to prevent birth control in the name of God do not show much compassion for the suffering of the unwanted children or the overstressed parents which this policy produces.

And there is plenty of foolishness on the other side too. When I was writing my master's thesis in seminary, I interviewed a number of fundamentalist pastors for a study I was doing on religious prejudice. I will never forget the response of one fellow who ran an independent church which he himself had organized. He told me that women aren't allowed to teach in his church because scripture forbids it. But, he said, if they studied with him and were willing to teach his doctrine, he would make an exception. Because, as he explained with a straight face, "If God could use an ass to do his will, I suppose he could also use a woman!"[11]

The church today is too often like a community club. It sponsors a great many social events which enrich the lives of its members. And it attempts to do good works in the area in which it exists. But when we get to the real business of the church, we are usually expected to listen to someone talk rather than having the opportunity to share with each other what God is doing in our lives. The church is generally closed to new ideas, especially the kinds of mystical experiences which it writes off as "new age." So those who are having life-changing spiritual experiences find the church unwilling to listen to their testimony. Rather, many are told that they are being manipulated by Satan. Is it any wonder that they leave the church to look for a fellowship that is more encouraging, more open to the Spirit?

When we consider our religious symbols – elaborate houses of worship, vestments, processions, clerical authority, and the expense of all this ostentation – and then think of how the early church conducted itself, we are forced to wonder what Jesus might think. Would he be amazed or appalled? Where has the simplicity gone?

The church is a socio/political human institution which has its own set of man-made rules. When the church excommunicates one of its members, that person is no longer in its club. But that club does not own the Kingdom of God. So it is perfectly possible to be part of the Kingdom and not be part of the club. And when enough of us live out the truth of that fact, it may force the club to reexamine itself and join the ever-growing spiritual awareness which is already enlightening the 21st century.

Chapter Nine

The Next Step

Now that we've spent all this time trying to demythologize the Christian religion, you might well ask what, if anything, are we going to put in its place? And that is an excellent question. In fact, if there were no answer to that question, the rest of this book would be pointless. We will deal at length with this question in Chapter 13.

But first, let me take the opposite point of view from what is expressed in the earlier chapters of the book. *There is a great deal that is right about the church.* I am not advocating that we get rid of Christianity. We could write many other books detailing all the positive things that the church has done over the last twenty centuries. The lives of the saints, for instance, are an excellent counter-balance to the wicked transgressions of the murderous popes. Millions of people have found nourishment for their souls, and courage in times of stress, from the faith which the church's message has inspired. The sick and helpless have been cared for when no other organization had the vision to minister to the need. The church has been the major factor, during the dark periods of history, in preserving the wisdom of the past. The presence of churches in towns everywhere has had a civilizing and uplifting effect on the populace. It's doubtful if the Civil Rights movement would have been as successful without the leadership of the church. And the church has been a primary inspiration for some of the greatest art and music of all time. So let us not forget that every issue has two sides, and the positive side of the church's heritage is a profound one.

But as time goes on, more and more people are going to realize that the emperor is naked, that they have been misled by a centuries-old fable. The fact is, we don't need to fear hell and we don't need to be "saved." So, while its mission is still valuable, the church's message needs to be updated. What I fear is that, as future generations come on the scene and people are less tied to the ancient worldviews, they are going to snicker at the church's gullibility and abandon it as anti-intellectual and irrelevant. If we are to preserve what is worth keeping about the church, we are going to have to make some dramatic changes in its theology.

The church leadership, as we have noted, issued a scholarly report in 1616 stating authoritatively that the Earth was the center of the solar system. The church was wrong. It mistook its own myth for the truth of God. That sort of thing has been happening all throughout history. And the issue we are discussing here is one more example of that fact. The church hierarchy can insist forever that its myth is historical fact, but time will prove that assertion to be wrong, just as it did in Galileo's case. The 21st century can no longer support a point of view so clearly medieval, a set of beliefs which belong in the same dustbin as The Flat Earth Society. There are still people who believe that the Earth is flat! Most of us see how ridiculous that claim is. How long will it take a majority of us to see that the church's claims are just as untenable?

When the church asserts that all scripture is literal fact, it uses a vast amount of its energy and credibility fighting a losing battle. When it insists that it is right and that those who disagree with it are wrong, it invites everyone to contest that claim. That leads to a struggle about whose "truth" is true and whose is false. And in that struggle, the love of Jesus gets trampled in the dust.

That's another imperative for making the single change that I am advocating. The church must take a giant leap forward and say publicly something like the following:

We have a lovely classic God-inspired story to tell you. It will help you understand that God loves, forgives and cherishes you. Our story is an ancient parable which will lead you to God, and when we get to heaven together, we will know the full story behind the parable.

When that happens, we will no longer be tempted to fight each other over the truth. Why? Because when we admit that our vision of heaven is mythological, we will finally understand the true value of myth. Myth is the sincere struggle of the human mind to express the inexpressible, to describe the indescribable, to make concrete the ineffable – in short, to do the impossible. And while our three-dimensional images may lead us in the direction of the 100-dimensional Kingdom of God, they will never reach that goal. That is why we must not cast them in concrete, because there is always a new truth just one step beyond where we are at the moment.

The myths of other religions will have a new kind of value for us, when we look on our own religious story as metaphor. Every other myth enlarges our own vision of the truth because each one is a small slice of the larger pie. When we get to that point, we will be liberated from having to insist, as our credulous forebears did, that every so-called miracle in the Bible is literally true. Then we can begin to unwrap the hidden meanings of the scriptural stories – their metaphorical truths – and use those truths to enhance our own spirituality. The consequence of all that will be nothing less than the elimination of the root cause of all religious wars.

Am I being naïve? Is it naïve to believe that Republicans and Democrats in Congress will one day abandon their childish, self indulgent wrangling, and begin to do what is good for the country, rather than simply what will get them re-elected? Is it naïve to think that the Kingdom of God is in the process of establishing itself on Earth? If we say yes to these questions, we will have handed the future to those who have no faith, no hope, no vision. And I don't want to live in that kind of world.

So…it is time for the church to shake off its medieval thinking and adopt an intellectual/spiritual approach which will fit it for dealing with the demands of the 21st century and beyond. The church's current message is in the form of myth, parable, metaphor and divine story. In the past, when we believed that those stories were fact, we felt the need to submit to the control of a religious hierarchy in order to be assured of attaining heaven. But in this modern age, the church needs to grow up. As I say on my website, *Beyond Religion*:[12]

> Organized religion is not the final truth in our search for God. Rather, it is the grammar school of faith, an important stage in our spiritual education but one from which we must eventually graduate.

I'm not talking about doing away with the Christian tradition. But we need to recognize that what the church is teaching now is the grammar school curriculum of spirituality – that we are sinners who need to be saved, that without faith in Jesus we are destined to hell, and that Christianity is the only true route to heaven. There is no question that we need the kindergarten of faith for our children, just as we need grammar school type lessons to inculcate basic spiritual principles in our young people. However, most people drop out of Sunday School around age twelve, if they attend at all, and thus they go through life with a junior high school level of understanding about spiritual things. So, at present, the church often pitches its message to its people as though it were speaking to eighth graders because that is all they are prepared to comprehend.

We must add high school and college level courses to the curriculum, more advanced subjects which will take into account the modern information which we are receiving in this new age of revelation. We do not have to abandon the past, but we do need to broaden the church's message with this new information. It's not something which should be forced on every member, just as we do not teach trigonometry to five-year-olds. But we must have the subjects available in the curriculum for members who are hungering for something more than the thin gruel of the church's traditional menu.

Deeply spiritual people, people who have spent their lives in sincere activity within the church, are having life-changing experiences which they see as coming from God. These glimpses of the divine are opening up a new awareness of how the physical and spiritual worlds interact, and they are providing answers to questions for which the church has never had satisfactory explanations. These bits of information are part of the "much more" that Jesus promised to tell us, through the mediation of the Holy Spirit.

The people who have had these experiences often want to share them with their pastor and their fellow members. But when they find that their stories are rejected, or when they are told that these things come from the devil, it is very confusing for them, deeply hurtful, and it forces them to choose between embracing their experience or listening to those who tell them to deny it. Is it any wonder that many of these people choose to leave the church rather than remain in an institution which talks about God but refuses to celebrate His activity in the lives of His people?

The church still operates on the basis of Paul's comment in I Cor. 3:2: "*I had to feed you milk, not solid food, because you were not ready for it. And even now, you are not ready for it.*" Well, many people in the pews *are* ready for something stronger than the milk of the gospel because, not only are they tired of hearing the same old stories repeated year after year, but they have a growing interest in these new topics. The world outside the church is becoming more familiar with spiritual issues, thanks to Hollywood films, television talk shows and the spiritual press. Many church members are not afraid of thinking for themselves, and they want a church which welcomes their curiosity rather than trying to discourage it.

The greatest resistance to this broader approach will come, as it always has, from the church professionals, those whose power and livelihood are wrapped up with the ancient traditions, and who therefore have the strongest motivation to keep those traditions intact. Thinking outside the box can get church leaders into serious trouble!

If these experiences are true, and if they come from God, why would we want to ignore them? In I John 4:1, we are told to test the spirits to see which ones come from God. I am the first to caution people that not every so-called "new truth from God" is legitimate. But by being overly cautious, we will certainly fail to notice many of the gifts that God has placed in our path. To hang on to the past for fear of the future is to live without faith because God can only be found in the present.

What kind of experiences am I referring to here? Let's talk about the most obvious one, the one which should be the easiest for the church to embrace: after-death communication (ADC). Millions of people have had visits from deceased loved ones. What these appearances demonstrate is totally in line with what religion has always taught. The church should therefore rejoice in the fact that there is now objective evidence that its central teaching is true: we have a soul which lives on in spirit form after we die.

What these experiences tell us, in addition, is that departed souls are able to interact with their loved ones who are still in physical form. We are reassured through these meetings that love transcends death, and that on the other side we continue to be aware, to grow and to care for those whom we love. Here is a story which illustrates this truth.

A Visit from Denise

When I was a junior in high school, I had a friend named Denise. She had been absent from school for several days when I decided to go visit her to see how she was feeling. We had a nice visit and she seemed well enough to return to school. She told me that she'd had a cold but now felt better, and that she'd be back at school the following day. I remember that she was smiling when she told me that.

That night I was asleep in my room when I awoke for no apparent reason. My dog, Duchess, was also awake and stood beside my bed looking toward the door to my room. I sat up in bed and looked toward the door. There, standing in the corridor facing my doorway, was Denise.

She was not misty or glowing or anything like that. She appeared to be just as real and whole as any living person. I did not feel any fear when I saw her, only mild confusion. I asked her what she was doing there in my house. She smiled and said, "I just wanted to stop and say goodbye."

I responded by saying "goodbye," but didn't ask her where she was going. My 16-year-old mind seemed satisfied with her answer. She turned as though she was going to walk on down the corridor toward the stairs, so I didn't see her disappear or fade away. After glancing at my alarm clock and noting that it was 4:30 a.m., I settled in and soon went back to sleep.

The next morning I thought about Denise's visit. It had not been a dream so I was at a loss to understand why she had been there. I decided to ask her about it when I saw her at school since she had said that she would be coming back that day.

But as soon as I got to school, another friend asked me if I had heard about Denise. I said no. Then she told me that Denise had died at 4:30 that morning. Her cold had suddenly developed into a severe form of pneumonia and she'd been rushed to the hospital where she had passed away. She had visited me before I knew that she was dead.

By visiting me, Denise gave me one of the best gifts that I have ever received, the gift of assurance that there is life after death and that we do go on. This knowledge has been a great comfort to me over the years.

Stories like that can have a profound impact on our thinking about who we are, what our connection is to the spirit world, and what lies in store for us. It also makes it clear that the spiritual side of life is not the exclusive possession of the religious community. In other words, we don't have to be religious to get into heaven! That other world is real, it is near to each of us, and it is as natural to move from here to there as it is to cross from one room in our house to another. Not only that, but there is a constant interaction between these two worlds, so that not only can those on the other side visit us, as in the case of Denise, but we can visit them through out-of-body experiences.

This knowledge, if it were to be seriously investigated by the religious leadership, and if it were incorporated into the church's statements of belief, could get rid of such misleading teachings as the idea that we have to wait for the second coming of Jesus before we can be raised from the dead. These modern experiences make it clear that some of the church's beliefs about death and the hereafter are wrong.

Embracing this truth about the next world would free people from the threat of excommunication because it would strip Peter of the keys with which to lock people out of heaven, and that would force the church to admit that it has no control over our souls. We would learn that our transition from this world to that other one is instantaneous, in line with what Jesus told the thief on the cross: "Today you will be in Paradise with me."

I hope that the church will not give up its will to live when it no longer has the power to threaten us with hellfire. If that is its only reason for being, then it needs to pass on. But if it begins to package its message in hope rather than fear, it will find a great many more people anxious to hear what it has to say.

One more story about an appearance from the other side. This one was submitted by Christine from Australia.

The "Moving" Picture

In 1991, my ten-year-old son Nicky was killed in a road accident. A few days before the accident, he told me that he didn't mind if he died young. In hindsight, it seemed as if he knew.

Following his death, our family experienced several visitations from Nicky. During the first week after he died, I felt him kiss me just as I woke up in the morning. In addition, I had several dreams in which he told me that he had important work to do where he was.

We had moved from the UK to New Zealand, and therefore our family was overseas and couldn't come to the funeral. Two weeks after the funeral, my husband's two sisters came to visit. We had the funeral service recorded on tape, so we started to show them the film. My husband and I and Nicky's older brother were also present.

As the service began, one of the sisters suddenly noticed that the picture of Nicky on the top of the TV was moving. As the five of us looked at it, Nicky's face came out of his picture in 3D. We could see him looking around the room and moving his head to do so. He was ecstatic. I had never seen him look so happy. He was talking to us but we couldn't hear any sound. We could lip read some of the words which were all positive. He was undoubtedly enjoying the whole experience. It seemed to us that he was trying to say that he now knew everything, and that it was fantastic.

This continued for quite a long time. Eventually, he faded back into the picture. We looked for the first time at the funeral service on the TV and it had come to an end. Later, we timed the tape and discovered that the five of us had witnessed Nicky's visit for over forty minutes. The sisters hadn't seen him for two years and weren't so emotionally involved, and this seemed further proof to us that it wasn't a mass illusion on our part.

The next day we wrote the experience down and we all signed it. This was in case we would think in later years that we had imagined the whole thing.

It is not imagination. It is a part of life, and church membership will be richer and more relevant when this truth becomes part of what the church teaches. After-death communication is a truth of God and, as seekers for God, we no longer need to be afraid of embracing this fascinating insight into our own future.

Chapter Ten

Angel Communication

Once we know that after-death communication is real, and that it proves to us that we continue to be alive and conscious after death, we can move on to Out-of-Body Experiences which demonstrate essentially the same thing – that we are a soul within a body, and that our soul can exist outside that body. The following story is an example of this phenomenon.

Traveling Outside the Car

This was the most memorable experience of my life. I have always believed that anything is possible but I had serious doubts about out-of-body experiences. A friend was driving me home from college one day.

About half an hour into our drive I fell asleep. I was enjoying the sun and the moving car, when I suddenly discovered that I was traveling outside the car. I saw the car moving and kept up with it, but I was aware that I was alongside my body which was still in the car. It was very peaceful and fulfilling, but all at once I got a little scared and wondered what was going on.

A minute later I was back in the car and in my body. I didn't know what to say to my friend because I knew she would think I was insane. I finally asked if anything had looked strange to her, and she said no.

A short time later I told this story to another friend, and he said that the same thing had happened to him and that it had also been spontaneous, not something he willed himself to do. I will never forget that experience for the rest of my life. It proved to me that if you can exist outside of your body, anything is possible.

Other things, such as dreams and visions are perfectly consistent with what we read in scripture. We need to make these subjects part of the church's curriculum. We also need to recover a belief in angels. The Bible is filled with angel activity, but the church has tended to downplay the subject, calling it an ancient superstition, outmoded in our day. Ironic, since the church doesn't think of itself as outmoded!

So, if the church can learn to promote itself as the custodian of a beautiful myth with deep metaphorical meaning, and if it can open its arms to a whole cluster of mystical experiences which demonstrate that the spirit world is our constant companion, it can begin a whole new age in its long life.

As we begin to make these changes in the church's belief system, we will find a God who is a whole lot more accessible than in the past. God is no longer hidden by the temple veil or the cathedral screen, or the pope or the squadrons of cardinals and bishops, or the armies of priests and pastors through whom we have always had to beg admittance to God's presence. God is here, within us, next to us, around, over and under us, closer than hands and feet, nearer even than breathing. We are never apart from God. We can talk to God in the daylight, meditate on Him in the darkness of our bedroom, write Him notes, send Him prayers, listen to His voice in our soul. Nothing separates us from God, and we are never out of His presence. We are part of God, and our name is the first name on His lips. We are submerged in God as a fish is one with the sea.

Now, we have no idea who God is or what God is like. The church, unfortunately, has too often simplified its image of God so that, while we may no longer think of Him as an old man with a long white beard, we do tend to use human images. So God ends up looking a lot like some kind of super-human personality, sitting on a cloud or something else up there, listening to prayers and holding a big book in which He records all of our actions, good and not so good.

But we know this is not accurate. God is more like a force field than a subject for anthropology. We can get dizzy thinking about the power that created the Big Bang and the incredible detail inside that explosion. How could any mind be big enough to plan or execute that unfathomable event?

The other question that makes *me* dizzy is pondering this question: Why does reality consist of the universe? Why does there have to be anything, any kind of existence? In other words, why isn't the natural state of reality simply a vast void of nothingness? Eternal unconsciousness? Which raises the question: Why does God exist? And what was God doing before the creation of the universe? We realize the mind-blowing fact that the universe has a life span – a beginning and an ending – but God doesn't! Where does God exist between the ending of one universe and the beginning of another?

Well, if this is making you dizzy too, let's move on. Is the God who made the universe the kind of entity which you would expect to find at the other end of your phone 24/7 answering all your prayers? I rather think not. But we can still believe that God is loving and supportive of our little lives, or He wouldn't have bothered to create us in the first place. So if God is the power of life in us, more of a cosmic generator than a customer service rep, then who is it who answers our calls when we phone in for help?

This is where angels and spirit guides come in. They are created beings, just as we are, and their purpose is to support, protect, encourage and, sometimes, even intervene to warn us of danger. The following story is one example.

An Angel Voice

My son, Dale Thomas, is now 27 and perfectly healthy. But he was an accident-prone child and this is the story of an "accident" that happened to him when he was two or three years old. It was spring or summer and that day my husband and I and our two sons went to a picnic in the park along with many other families connected with my husband's softball team.

One of the other ladies had just had a baby girl, who was not even two weeks old, and while all the kids were playing I was talking to her. I asked if I could hold her baby. I was totally focused on this conversation and had not a worry in mind. As she stretched out her arms to hand me her baby, a loud voice yelled in my head - "WHERE ARE YOUR KIDS?" It was a male voice and sounded extremely desperate and upset. I immediately stopped reaching for the baby and said, "Wait a minute. I have to find my kids."

I started visually panning the park looking for my boys. At about the one o'clock position I saw my older son, Adam, who was four or five years old, sitting on the grass playing with some other children. He appeared to be fine.

I continued looking for my other son, Dale. As I turned all the way around, I saw, very far away where the slides were, a child lying on the ground at the bottom of the steps of the 10-foot slide! This child, my son Dale, lifted up his head and opened his mouth, then dropped his head to the ground. He had fallen off this huge 10-foot slide to the hard cement below.

I immediately started running as fast as I could towards him. When I picked him up, his beautiful blue eyes had no pupils and he started vomiting. At the hospital, it became clear that Dale had fallen on his head and had a severe concussion.

He made a full recovery and later told us that another child had been on the steps of the slide above him, and that dirt had fallen into Dale's eyes. He let go of the slide to wipe his eyes and fell to the bottom, hitting his head on the cement. I can imagine that if that voice had not alerted me, Dale could easily have choked on his own vomit.

I am totally convinced this was divine intervention and I am so thankful for it. Some people might say that it was just my motherly instinct kicking in. I respond, "If this was me talking to myself, why didn't the voice say, 'Where are my kids?'" No, this male voice said, "Where are your kids??!!" Also, since I work in the mental health field, I do not hear voices in my head regularly and I do know the difference.

There is more out there than what meets the eye! There is a spiritual life, and I look forward one day to meeting this "male" and thanking him properly for saving my son's life.

We need to regain the knowledge that angels are an intimate part of our daily existence. There are countless books on the subject on the religion shelves of bookstores these days. Our website has a whole section on angel communication. Here is a particularly beautiful story.

An Angel of Light

When I was 16 years old, I was in my bed one night next to a window. I looked up at the sky and marveled at how vast the universe was and yet how lonely it seemed. I started talking to God, telling Him how I felt. I had begun to wonder if God really existed because of all the pain in the world. How could it be God's "will" for my neighbor, a little girl of twelve, to be confined in a wheelchair for her entire life while I could run, dance and do cartwheels? This made no sense to me.

What about all the times I had prayed for my dad to stop drinking? Nothing had changed. I asked, "Don't you hear me God? Have you ever? Why, oh why do we have young boys fighting in Viet Nam? Why the Holocaust?" How could He allow all these atrocities if He was so powerful and loved us so much?

I cried hot tears as I talked. I told Him that if He didn't exist, I would rather not have been born. What would be the purpose? Just to live and die? And that ached my heart so much it was like a hand crushing it. I told Him that if I were He I would, with a wave of my hand, take all the pain from the world. There would be no hunger, no wars, no sickness, only love. So, why didn't He do all this if he was so powerful? I poured out my heart to Him until I was completely spent. I had had my say and I was done.

Suddenly I felt as though someone was watching me. I raised my head to look around but no one was there. The feeling became more intense and I raised my head up higher. And much to my absolute surprise a bright light was bouncing along my ceiling.

I sensed a feminine essence. She was astoundingly beautiful, a circular light with no edges or boundaries, She was intensely bright and twinkling like millions of diamonds or Fourth of July sparklers, only much, much brighter. Yet the light didn't hurt my eyes. And her light cast no shadows as she bounced along my ceiling. She appeared to be about the size of a basketball and I could sense eternity within her light.

I felt in awe of what I was seeing. I had not asked for a sign. I had been taught that to ask for a sign was a sin. So, this was most unexpected. I sensed her message: "Be joyful! God has heard you! He loves you! You are precious to Him!" All this and more was wrapped up in her love-filled light. It was like she was dancing, dancing with joy. And I felt her joy – she gave me her joy.

I had absolutely no doubt that I was wide awake. I knew immediately that what I saw was actually happening and that it was real. I watched for a few moments and then squeezed my eyes shut. When I opened them again, she was gone. Still, I knew she had been real.

I jumped from my bed, ran to my mom's bedroom and woke her from a sound sleep. I was crying tears of joy as I told her, "Mom! God was in my bedroom!"

After that, I had no doubts about God – whether He existed and if He heard my prayers. Later, I realized it wasn't actually God who had appeared to me. He had sent a messenger, an Angel of Light. I was truly blessed that night.

Whenever I flounder or have doubts, even to this day, I remember that night and I know that God is real, that He hears our prayers and that He is with us.

Angels come in all forms, sometimes totally unexpected ones. A woman in my congregation took a dislike to me for some reason and quit coming to church. For years she kept her distance, letting me know that I had incurred her displeasure. Nothing I did was successful in healing the breach between us. So you can imagine my surprise when she appeared in my study one day and announced that she had a message for me from Jesus!

My wife and I had lost a baby at full term some five years before this meeting. We already had two daughters and had decided that we didn't want to risk another pregnancy after our loss. But this woman, who sat next to the door as if prepared for a quick escape, announced that we were going to have another baby, that it would be a boy, and that he would be healthy. And then she left.

We were flabbergasted! Just that morning, my wife had told me she thought she might be pregnant. She was, and the prophecy, the message from Jesus, came true in every detail. This woman's words gave us complete peace of mind during the pregnancy, and were a true gift from God. But His choice of a messenger – an angel – always mystified and amused us.

Let me talk briefly about numerology as a channel for connection with our angels. The numbers 111 or 1111 have fairly recently come to be seen as "angel numbers," numbers which, when we see them unexpectedly, alert us to be aware of our angels or guides. Go online and search for "1111" and you will find thousands of sites which have stories to tell about the heavenly significance of these numbers.

Some time ago, I began seeing the number 1111 when I was under stress, worried about something, anxious about an upcoming event. More often than not, I would see the number on a digital clock, or on a passing truck, or as a file number that I accidentally came across. It happened more often than could be accounted for by chance, and it always brought me a sense of relief and comfort. When we accept this phenomenon as a channel through which our angels can contact us, we begin to see it more often, and each sighting strengthens the link between us. Each time I see it, I remember that my angels are working hard for me, still pumping faithfully in that boat above my head.

When I was writing about angel communication in my previous book, *A Handbook For Heretics*, I was deeply concerned about how this idea would be received by my readers. Was I foolish to think that people would take it seriously? While I was pondering the wisdom of including the subject in the book, the phone rang. It was a woman whose wedding I had performed a number of years earlier. I had not seen her since then, and she had no idea what I was doing or what my interests were. She told me that something unusual was happening to her, and she didn't know who else to consult about it. She said, "Every time I look at the clock, it says...," and my mind raced ahead, waiting for her to say something like "2:49." She finished by saying: "11:11." I literally fell off my chair laughing. She must have thought that I was making fun of her, but the timing of her call was an incredible gift to me. It was my angel telling me, "Now, how much clearer can we make this? Do you believe us now??"

I must mention a phenomenon known as the Christ Spirit. Who that Spirit is, is a mystery, but it helps reveal how God interacts with human beings. The Christ Spirit can be viewed as a super-angel, or perhaps the heavenly version of royal jelly. In the bee world, a substance called royal jelly is used in heavy doses to create queen bees, although small amounts are fed to all the larvae in the hive. Thus, while all of us are filled with the Holy Spirit, the Christ Spirit, far more potent, enters certain ordinary individuals and causes them to become extraordinary prophets. Thus, there is a difference between Jesus of Nazareth and The Christ of God. Jesus was a man, but when the Christ Spirit descended on him, he became something much more, a queen bee among workers, so to speak, a person so advanced that people were inspired to call him the Son of God.

But Christians do not own the Christ Spirit any more than they own the Holy Spirit. That special anointing power of God was in all the great avatars of history, and it will be in others yet to be born. This makes it clear that there is one God and that the inspiration behind all religions is the same spirit, the spirit of the Christ – which means "the anointed one" – for lack of a more universal name, as distinct from the Jesus of history.

People who have had near-death experiences report being met by a Being of Light, a personality so brilliant and loving that they were overwhelmed by it. Depending on their religious background, they called it by different names. Christians, of course, call it Jesus. But by separating Jesus of Nazareth from the Christ Spirit, we can avoid having to think of Jesus as sitting on a throne alongside of God. Jesus was the human who died. Jesus' spirit appeared to his disciples and then ascended into heaven. The Christ Spirit, however, departed from him at his death and has continued to inspire other avatars in the centuries since then.

If we allow our minds to be open, we can see divine activity in many areas of our life. The world's mantra is: Seeing is Believing. But in the world of spirit, just the opposite is true: Believing is Seeing. Once we let God guide us, rather than being held captive by our rational mind, we see things we didn't know existed.

The servant of Elisha had this experience in II Kings 6. He and Elisha were surrounded by an enemy army at Dothan, and the servant despaired, certain that they were going to be killed. But Elisha prayed: *" 'O Lord, open his eyes and let him see!' The Lord answered his prayer, and Elisha's servant looked up and saw the hillside covered with horses and chariots of fire all around Elisha."*

Those horses and chariots of fire still surround us today, if we have the eyes of faith with which to see them.

Chapter Eleven

Reincarnation

I want to spend an entire chapter on the subject of reincarnation, since it is an essential element of this new worldview which we are trying to establish. And reincarnation is probably the one idea which most clearly distinguishes it from traditional Christian dogma.

The common viewpoint of the church is that reincarnation is incompatible with biblical teaching because of Hebrews 9:27: *"Everyone must die once, and after that be judged by God."* The teaching about the resurrection of the body must be abandoned if we possess many bodies over time: the question then becomes, which body will be ours in the judgment? This is because Christian theology teaches that after the judgment the soul is either eternally rewarded with heaven, or eternally punished in hell.

But the idea of rebirth removes all the ammunition from the church's gun on that issue. If we have an unlimited number of opportunities to "get it right," then the church can no longer threaten us with hellfire because of our misdeeds in this present life, and it loses its power to control its people. That ecclesiastical power is dependent on the one-life worldview which gives the leadership the ability to manipulate people through fear. The concept of rebirth, however, gets rid of the idea of eternal punishment or reward, and replaces it with unlimited future physical lives. This puts the individual soul out of reach of the church authorities. So it's no wonder that the Christian leadership has opposed the idea for most of the church's history.

I say "most" because one of the greatest of the Church Fathers, Origen, left the door open for reincarnation when he carefully worked out a theology which taught the pre-existence of the soul. If his teachings had been allowed to become part of church dogma, Christianity would have been teaching reincarnation almost from the start. But it was not to be. Political considerations resulted in a papal decision around the sixth century banning the teaching of reincarnation. That became the position of the church, not because the idea of reincarnation was false, but because it did not fit in with the theological position of the church. Again, the church was putting politics before truth, as it did later with Galileo. Today the idea of reincarnation is dismissed by the church because it is considered an "eastern" doctrine. The irony is that Christianity began as a Middle Eastern religion!

Before we move along, it should be noted that there are several references in the New Testament which show that the disciples of Jesus took for granted the idea of rebirth. Jesus asked them on one occasion who people said that he was, and they responded, *"Some say John the Baptist,... others say Elijah, while others say Jeremiah or some other prophet."*[13] Now, interestingly, all these men were dead, indicating that his followers believed it was possible for people to be reborn.

In Chapter 2, we mentioned the man who had been blind from birth. Jesus' disciples asked, *"Teacher, whose sin caused him to be born blind? Was it his own or his parents' sin?"*[14] The assumption here was that this man was being punished in his present life for sins committed in a past life. Since he had been born blind, the sins for which he was being punished could not have been committed in his current life. So the Bible itself is certainly open to the idea of rebirth and, in this last case, even to the existence of karma.

We are saying that there is nothing but God, so that everything which is created, including ourselves, is part of God, made from the essence of God's own nature. That means that we have always existed with God. Quite aside from asking why God created us – or why He created anything, for that matter – we need to be clear about what we have been doing since the beginning of time.

There is a saying that in heaven, we know but we don't grow, while on Earth, we can grow but we don't know. While we are in the spirit world, we know the meaning of existence and so we know who we are and who God is. But that knowledge comes easily on the other side. For our soul to truly grow, we need to learn these lessons from our own hard-earned experience. And so, to enable that growth, we come here where we are screened from the knowledge we had in heaven, and the memories of our past lives are blocked from our conscious mind.[15] But that awareness is buried in our souls, and our job here is to allow it to come to the surface so that we may gain wisdom and help the world become the Kingdom of God on Earth.

There is a beautiful parable contained in a little book called *Christ In Me*. It concerns a seed planted in the earth. The seed is buried in the dark soil because it seems to be dead and dead things need to be buried. But then something remarkable happens. The seed begins to sprout feelers – roots and shoots. And no matter what position it was buried in, its shoot knows to reach upwards. That is the miracle in the heart of the seed. In the darkness where it was buried, it knows how to reach for the light. And this is because it was created by the sun, and the memory of the sun is still alive in the heart of the seed. So it reaches out for reunion with the sun from where its life came.

That is a metaphor for our relationship with God. We are planted in the darkness of Earth, away from the light in which we were created. But the light still remains in our hearts, and our task here is to learn to reach upward for reunion with the light of God. In heaven we may have head knowledge, but we are here to learn soul knowledge from the difficult lessons our physical experience offers us.

Another way to look at it is that we are extensions of God, projections of living energy with which He reaches out to learn and grow. He puts us here together in order to learn how we respond to the various stimuli that life affords. And each bit of knowledge that we gain informs Him, expands His wisdom, enlarges His reality, so that He becomes ever larger, wiser and more creative. Life is change; death is the lack of change. God is life, so even He is ever-changing. And we are His fingertips with which He feels His way into a larger future. We come here to learn, after which we return to report on what we have gained. Then we can choose to continue our personal growth and our work for God. We are an important part of the creation process, and that process will continue forever. And so the options we have for new lives, new experiences, are unlimited.

Many people have recalled scenes from their former lives. Children especially are in touch with their previous life because the subconscious memory of that experience has not yet been replaced by the activities of their new life. It takes about seven years to become acclimated to their new identity, so until that time they may suddenly blurt out a statement which refers to a former experience. Following are five short examples of this phenomenon.

My Grandson's Former Life?

When my grandson was six he liked to tell his mother, "Mommy, you're beautiful." He would tease his father, who is several years older than his mother, and say, "Daddy, you're old!" Then he would giggle. It was at a time when he was expressing certain concepts he was growing to understand, such as age and relationships. He would say things to me like, "You're my grandmother. You're my mom's mother." For whatever reason, he felt the need to state these understandings out loud and directly to us.

One day he was staying with me and he told me, "Grandma, you're old!" I agreed with him immediately because I knew that to him I was "old" even though I was in my early fifties and quite fit. Then he paused and became very serious. In an entirely different tone and attitude he looked at me and said, "I used to be an old man. Then I was a baby, and now I'm a boy."

He was thoughtful when he made that comment, serious rather than joking, as though he was remembering something right then and feeling the memory. It was stated very casually. Prior to that, he had just been poking fun at me. But when he said he had been an old man, then a baby, and now a boy, he said it in a matter-of-fact way, like he was giving me real information, and also telling me, "I used to be like you."

Coming Back as a Baby

The other day, my four-year-old daughter asked me if, when she comes back as a baby again, she could have the same baby toys. I asked her what she meant, and she explained: "When I die and come back as a baby again."

I was flabbergasted. We are not a religious family and have never even discussed the concept of reincarnation in our home. I asked her where she came up with the idea, and she further explained that she just "felt it" in her heart.

I truly feel my daughter has an older soul. She came out of the womb literally wide-eyed and moving her head to look around. She began speaking at the age of one and spoke so well that, when we were out, strangers would stop and comment in disbelief at how well she spoke for her age.

She's made me think twice about what happens after we die. As science explains, matter and energy can't be destroyed; they are just transformed. □

He Was A Little Girl

At the beginning of September 1990, I dreamt of my father who had died in January 1990. In the dream, my father was with a little girl who was crying, and he was trying to comfort her. He told her that I was to be her grandmother and I would look after her. So I was convinced that my daughter, who was pregnant at the time, would have a little girl. However, to my surprise, it turned out to be a little boy.

Three years after the child was born, I was on a bus with him. When we passed a certain park, he instantly recognized it and told me that he had died there. However, he was not a boy at the time but a little girl. He said that he had run out into the road when his mummy had told him not to. I was amazed at his story. He repeated it three more times and the details never changed.

One day I was visiting my nephew's wife, and I told her the story. She looked up in shock and said, "I remember when I was at secondary school in that area, there was a little girl killed in a road accident. It was in the local newspaper."

A Child's Frightening Memory

Ever since my son was very young, he has always been scared of the shower. Every time I take him near the shower, he screams and cries.

When he was four years old, he came to me and told me a story that sent chills down my spine and made me cry. That afternoon I had asked him, "Why don't you take a shower today instead of a bath?" He replied, "I don't want to die, Mommy."

I asked, "What are you talking about?"

He answered, "I died in the shower with my other mommy." I asked him again what he was talking about, and he said very clearly, "The army men made me and Mommy go in the shower with all the other people, and we died."

The first thing that came to my mind was the horror of the Holocaust, but we have never allowed him to watch anything on television dealing with the Holocaust. He still is adamant about not going in the shower, and sometimes he tells me little details which are impossible for him to know.

For instance, he says that he had "boo boo's" all over his body that itched all day, and that he always got yelled at for scratching them. I've heard of the horrible body lice that people in the concentration camps had to endure. He also talks about dogs. He is scared to death of dogs and says he was bitten by a dog on his leg. The area where he says he was bitten has a birthmark.

The Memory of a Fire

I was cleaning my then six-year-old daughter Talisa's room when I spotted a small luggage-type case under her bed. I decided I'd take a peek at what was inside. When I opened the box, I was shocked to see that, in addition to a few of her favourite items - photos and small trinkets - she was also saving some non-perishable types of food.

I called her upstairs to explain what all this stuff, especially the food, was doing in her case. She said that it was all she needed in case we had to leave in a hurry because of a fire. I tried to reassure her that we would get her out safely in case of a fire, that we had alarms and so on, anything that would put her mind at ease. But she insisted that she really needed all these things.

I asked her why she was so afraid, and was shocked to hear her response. She said that when she was Sally she was sleeping in her house, and she died in a fire. I said, "No, your name is Tali and you're fine." (We sometimes called her Tali and I thought she was confusing the name with Sally.)

She then went on to tell me of a vivid recollection. She had been a child about seven years old who lived on a farm. Her house was built of wood and she slept on the top floor. One night, there was a big fire. She was trapped upstairs and nobody could get to her. The fire began coming through the floorboards and her long white nightgown started to burn. In desperation, as she tried to put out her flaming nightgown, she jumped out of a window, but died of her burns anyway.

What is most bizarre about it is that she has vitiligo all over her body (white patches). Many people have told me that they originally thought that those patches were the scars resulting from burns.

Let me add two stories of past-life recalls from adults.

Killed by the Nazis?

Ever since I can remember, I have been obsessed with World War II and the Holocaust. When I was about four years old, long before I knew about those events, I began to have a recurring vision just as I was falling asleep.

I would hear the sound of soldiers marching on the street. It was night and I was on the ground with my face lying against the cold wet cobblestones. I saw black boots marching in unison past me. My eyes would stay fixated on the boots, and I would have the feeling that I was about to die.

This vision was constant and for about twenty years it never changed. I remember lying in my bed and hearing the marching soldiers echoing in my head. My parents have told me that at night I would run into their room crying, begging my mom to "make the German soldiers stop marching."

I am 23 years old now, and only have the vision every few months. Nor do I hear the marching as often. But I have a strong urge to know more about the Holocaust, about my past, and to find out what the dream means. I have always had this nagging feeling that I was killed in the Holocaust.

I read a book written by a man who survived the Holocaust. In it he said that "No person dead or alive who was there (in the Holocaust) will ever forget the sound of the Nazi soldiers marching."

A Fear of Horses

I have always had a fear of horses I couldn't explain. I have gone horseback riding many times in an attempt to overcome that fear. I always figured that I was intimidated by them simply because they were so big in comparison to myself. I couldn't understand why even the most docile horses would inexplicably react weirdly around me. On two occasions, they actually bolted while I was on board, as though they sensed my fear. I was forever fighting this fear, but I had no idea where it came from.

Then, I had a spontaneous past-life recall. I remembered a time when I was walking down a covered boardwalk in a small town somewhere, perhaps the "old west." I recall walking on the wooden slats that formed the sidewalk, and realizing that you had to step down a good foot into the main street, which was merely a dirt road through the tiny town I lived in.

I was aware that while I was under the overhang in front of the row of shops, I was out of the hot noonday sun, and it was a welcomed relief. Still, I needed to cross the street on the diagonal to greet a man, whom I took to be my husband at the time. I was wearing a full hooped skirt with a tight bodice, and I believe I wore a bonnet.

In my excitement to greet him, I stepped down off the boardwalk, and was immediately struck down by a stage coach with a team of six horses. I looked to my left as I took a step or two into the street, then realized that it was inevitable that I would be struck.

I don't recall being hit, but I certainly remember the fear that I felt for the millisecond before I was trampled to death. I am sure that the entire team and the stagecoach ran over me. That spontaneous recall helped me to understand my lingering fear of horses.

There are literally thousands of these stories from all over the world in books being written these days. It is difficult to write off all of them as imagination, or to dismiss them as meaningless dreams. It seems to me that the evidence is growing more convincing daily that we live multiple lives, and that those lives are valuable to us and to God.

Chapter Twelve

Other Mystical Experiences

In the previous chapters, we've spoken about angel communication, out-of-body experiences, after-death communication, and reincarnation. What other types of experiences does the church need to learn to embrace?

On our site, we have been collecting stories from around the world for a number of years, and we find that these accounts fall into ten different categories. The other six include: Coincidence, Near-Death Experiences, Pre-Birth Experiences, Meditating, Healing, and Dreams and Visions.

I am particularly interested in the memories which some people have of the period before their birth. These glimpses of the spirit world by a soul before it incarnates give further evidence that we have always existed and that we have lived previous lives. Here are two of those stories.

A Pre-Birth Premonition

I was eight months pregnant with my son, Hank Alan Johnson. I was in bed when I heard the windows in the front door rattle like someone had just come in. I heard footsteps across the kitchen floor and down the hall, and they came up to the post at the foot of my bed.

The person standing there looked like my husband. But then I noticed that he was younger, had brown eyes and brown hair, but the same features. It was then I realized it was not my husband. As soon as I thought this, he turned and walked back down the hall, across the kitchen and out the door, rattling the window glass again.

I got up and checked the door and found that the chain was still on it. I called my husband at work and asked if he had been home and he said no. I started to look around the house, but there was no one anywhere.

We went to the doctor's to get a sonogram. She said it was a girl. But I told her it was a boy, that he would have brown hair and brown eyes and would look just like my husband. Sure enough, when he was born it was all true. After he was able to walk, he would get up in the night and come to my bed post. I would ask him if he was ok, and he would say yes, and I would put him back to bed.

He continued to come and stand at my bedpost up into his 20's. I was afraid it was a sign that something was going to happen to him at a young age. I was very careful, but after he turned 14 and on up I became less worried. Then on July 10, 2008 he was robbed, beaten and injured so badly that he was in the CCU in a coma for eleven days. He died on July 21, 2008. He was 27 and had 2 kids.

My nightmare premonition that I always dreaded had come true.

Memories Before I Was Born

I remember distinctly before being born, that while I was waiting patiently for the vehicle (body) I would use, my future mother had an abortion. I felt very sad. But I overheard a couple talking about having a baby. I could see them, could see what they were wearing and where they were.

The site was located in Havana, Cuba. Between the old zoo and a place called The Forest of Havana, there is a park with benches. At the time, I was suspended above the couple and I could hear their conversation very clearly. Afterwards, I sensed how much they loved each other and how much they wanted a baby. I could feel their emotion internally. I decided I wanted to be with them although we were going to go through some hardships. At the moment I made that decision, I felt as though a vacuum sucked me in, and it was like I went to sleep until a couple of days after I was born.

After being born, I remember that I tried to speak but all I could hear were screams. Then I saw the face of my present mother and guessed she was the one I saw that day. Once I could physically talk in this life, I told my parents about the experience. When I told them the story, they remembered being at the zoo, but could not remember what they were wearing. I went to the closet and took out the clothes. They went into shock when they realized that I recalled their exact conversation.

When I was sixteen, I met a friend of my mother's who came to the house. I recognized her immediately as the woman who was supposed to be my mother but who had had the abortion. I told her about the man who would have been my father and about her abortion. She couldn't believe what I was saying, but because there were so many details, there was not a doubt in my mind. We remained friends and her daughter from a later marriage always thought of me as her brother.

Actually, I consider myself very lucky to have a relationship with both my actual mother and the previous one. The reason for this experience, and being able to prove it to witnesses, is to demonstrate to the world that life goes on regardless of bodily death.

Another kind of experience which has always fascinated me is coincidence. It has been said that coincidence is the technique God uses when He wants to remain anonymous. It is an example of an important spiritual law, the Law of Attraction. The more we can learn about this law, the more we will be able to understand some of the remarkable events which until now have been inexplicable.

The story I want to use here is one that happened to me. It is so incredibly unlikely, so carefully worked out in time, that it must have been arranged by some purposeful intelligence. It always brings me joy and amazement when I think about it.

Meeting Evelyn

In 1988 I made a trip east to bring our son, David, home from New York City after his sophomore year at NYU. I took our daughter, Laurie, along for company on the long trip, which takes eight hours. Laurie was married and expecting their first child.

The night before the trip, I dreamt about Evelyn. Evelyn had been our next door neighbor during all my childhood years. She was like a second mother and still lived in the same house in New Jersey where I had known her. I don't remember ever dreaming about her before.

As we were traveling through New Jersey the next day, Laurie noticed that we were going to pass close to my old hometown, Cranford. She suggested that we stop briefly to see some of the spots she had visited as a child when her grandparents were still living there. So we drove through town quickly, and I showed her my old high school and some other spots of interest, including the homes of some of my former girlfriends! Then we drove down the main street to see the church I had attended in my youth.

Laurie asked, "Do you think we could stop to see Evelyn?" I said, "I'd like to, but we could only stay five minutes, and it wouldn't be fair to drop by unannounced for such a short visit." So, reluctantly, we decided to continue on without seeing her.

We were already late, but Laurie wanted to see one more place, the spot down by the river where she had fed the ducks when she was a child. So we drove to the area and turned left to cross a bridge over the river. I planned to make another left turn at the next street and go in by the opposite side of the river where the ducks congregated. But I discovered that the town fathers had changed the street to one-way, the wrong way. So I said to Laurie, "We'll go down to the next street and come back around the block."

As I started to turn left at the second street, I had to wait for two women who were crossing the intersection. As we drove behind them, I asked Laurie, "Who does that look like?" and she said, "It looks like Evelyn." And it was. We jumped out of the car and had a wonderful five-minute reunion right there on the sidewalk, a mile from her home.

We had left western Pennsylvania eight hours earlier and driven 400 miles to arrive at that precise spot in New Jersey at that exact moment to see the one individual about whom I had dreamt the night before. We could have missed that meeting for any number of reasons: If we had gone to her house, if the first street had not been one-way, if we had stopped on the road one time more or less, even if we had been thirty seconds sooner or later for any reason. Some intelligence had worked out the details perfectly.

Evelyn later told me that she and her companion were an hour and a half late taking their walk that day because of her busy schedule.

There is one additional category that I want to include here – Dreams and Visions. We all know that dreams can contain important messages for us, but they are so often scrambled that they seem meaningless, and because they are dreams it is easy to simply ignore them.

But visions are a different type of experience. The person is awake and sees something which is not physical, not part of the concrete world around them. These events give evidence that we can see into the spirit world on special occasions, and that entities on the other side can project messages to us through this medium. Visions show us another connection between our two worlds.

Something Special for Me

My husband died by suicide at our Arizona home on the tenth of March, 1997. His body was cremated and the family returned to Michigan for his memorial service.

The third week of April, I was sitting in my summer apartment in Michigan quietly reading a book with quite fine print. I was intent on the text.

As I was reading, the printed letters left the open pages of the book. Along the upper left corner appeared a patch of green grass and I could see our lawn area as if I were looking through the window of the attached front porch of my apartment.

As the green lawn area grew larger, I could see a moving figure appear wearing a black baseball cap with the initials AJ above the brim. I gradually realized that this was my husband, striding slowly across the lawn wearing a blue plaid western shirt and light blue jeans. These were favorite articles of clothing for him, including his Apache Junction cap.

This vision continued in color, as he walked toward his left, stepping higher up as if onto the front steps to the porch. Through the window, I could see my husband stand quietly looking to his left, the full side of his face appearing as healthy and rosy complexioned as ever he had been in his lifetime. As he turned his face towards me, I could see he was also wearing his large, fancy western belt buckle.

As quickly as it had all appeared on the pages of the book before me, it all disappeared. The printed lettering returned to the book in my lap. I sat in shock; it had all happened in seconds. Unable to explain this to myself, I realized that my prayers had been answered. He had been sent so that I would know he was OK.

Dreams have the power to point us to God's plan for us, to warn us, to show us the future, to give us comfort and reassurance. As I said, it is easy to ignore them, but certain dreams come with their own validation. These dreams have to be taken more seriously because they reveal an important connection to the spirit world, and so we should not be afraid to investigate their meaning. The Bible is full of dreams which are messages from God. In some cultures, it is common to sit around the breakfast table and compare dreams from the night before, helping family members unravel their meaning.

A Shared Dream

On January 3, 2005, I dreamt that I was walking on a path along the shores of a beach which I felt was in Jamaica where I'm from originally. The path was not paved, but instead was covered with white gravel stones and led to a small wooden beach house featuring a verandah with a door and a window on the right.

I walked up two or three steps from the ground to the verandah and, just as I got there, I turned around and saw a colleague of mine from work. He was walking up the same path and joined me on the landing. I asked what he was doing there but I don't recall his response. After he joined me, we both entered the house and went into a room where we found a middle-aged Caucasian woman. She presented me with a folded-up white cloth. I recall my friend looking on, smiling, and he seemed very pleased with the proceedings.

I awoke after that and went to work the next day, for the most part forgetting about the dream. This all changed a few days later when the same colleague and I were walking towards the elevators. He casually asked me, "So, when are you going to tell me about your dream?"

I replied, "What dream?" He said, "You had a dream a couple of days ago. We were together on a beach." I turned to him and asked, "How do you know this?" He started chuckling and asked what else I remembered, to which I replied, "The white lady."

He then said, "Don't you remember, she gave you something?" I replied, "A towel, I think" He then said, "She gave you a white robe – this is a good thing. It means you're on the right path and now you know what you must do." This experience was a confirmation for me of the existence of a spiritual realm.

Since that event, my whole attitude toward religion has shifted to a spiritual interpretation of what God is. As I try to figure out what "I must do," the experience has been invaluable to me in providing the comfort of knowing there is more to this world than we can see.

All of these various mystical experiences have a definite spiritual dimension to them. We wonder, therefore, why the church is so reluctant to see them as part of God's revelation, in the same category with scripture and prophesy. If sharing these experiences could become a normal part of the worship program of the church, our spiritual life would be vastly enriched, and people would lose their fear of opening up to the mystical side of life. These stories should be a gift to the whole community, something to be shared, an encouragement to others to believe that we live in a spiritual milieu, and that we are companioned by loving entities whose job it is to protect us, to guide us, and to remind us of who we really are.

Chapter Thirteen

Moving from Theology to Spirituality

In this final chapter, we will try to answer the question which has been generated by everything we have said up to this point: What will take the place of traditional religion? We can't just blow the church out of the water and then hope that the world will continue to function as if nothing had happened. Religious thinking and praxis are central to our culture; they have an important role to play in encouraging positive civil behavior, spiritual aspiration, cooperation with others, and respect for authority. To remove this important constraint on undisciplined behavior could have disastrous consequences.

Therefore, it's essential that we design something of equal, or even superior, value to put in its place. This displacement will not take place all at once. It will follow an evolutionary course, and will develop gradually as more and more people see its value for them personally and support its role in society. As it grows organically, this new form of spiritual practice will in time displace the older more traditional forms, just as equal rights for women and minorities is slowly overcoming the outmoded perception that Caucasian men alone should have their rights protected by law. The world is changing, and those changes will eventually do away with mythological belief systems. It is essential, therefore, that this new approach be put in place to provide a smooth transition as we let go of the old way of practicing spirituality. We will always need some kind of spiritual institution to help society seek the betterment of humankind.

What will that new system look like? What will we do in place of sitting in a pew on Sunday morning and listening to a sermon, or sitting through the traditional mass one more time? How can these new ideas about God be worked into a kind of group behavior which not only makes sense and inspires, but at the same time delivers a more accurate understanding of spiritual reality?

The Worship Service

The most obvious place to begin is corporate worship. This is the central image of what religion is all about, a group of believers gathered in a house of prayer to worship God together. In this setting, traditional beliefs which have been passed down for two millennia are reinforced by weekly rituals.

Now, since we recognize that much of the content of those gatherings is a mythological description of the nature and will of God, there will have to be some changes. We will no longer think of Jesus as God; we will not have altar calls during which we are urged to accept him as our savior; we will not hear preaching about how to avoid hellfire when we die; we will realize that transubstantiation is just one more myth, that the elements of bread and wine do not change into the body and blood of Jesus. As a result, we will no longer be drawn to worship out of fear of God's judgment. So, what will there be left to do in worship?

Well, to the casual observer, there won't be a whole lot of difference. The pageantry of divine worship can have a strong uplifting effect on our souls, and I would hate to be without it. Organ music, processionals, choral anthems, baptism, the Lord's Supper, congregational hymn singing, corporate prayers – these are all things that nurture our souls. And we can continue to observe them all, so long as they are set in a context which is consistent with all that we now know about spiritual reality. *The main difference will be that we have moved from theology to spirituality.*

The Sermon

The most basic change, in our effort to move from theology to spirituality, will be a change in the style of preaching. So much of religion in the past has been based on fear – fear of God, fear of hell, fear of accepting our own human nature, fear of making mistakes, fear of breaking the laws of God. Preachers have for ages capitalized on these fears and used them to manipulate their people into what they consider to be proper behavior.

But in this new age, fear is to be replaced by a sense of mature responsibility. We believe in a friendly and welcoming God who wants to work with us to make life as productive and joyful as possible. We do the right thing, not because we are afraid of God or hell, but because it *is* the right thing, because it creates the kind of society that we want to live in, because it fills life with the love of God.

So, to begin with, hellfire preaching will be gone, consumed in the flames of its own fears. The idea of scaring people into righteousness by the threat of eternal punishment will be recognized as an immature hangover from former days. Gone also will be heavy theological preaching which merely recounts the old beliefs, telling people what they must believe, declaring that this belief system is the only one that will get them into heaven.

So, how does the preacher change his style to reflect this new vision of God's truth?

Storytelling

Well, Jesus told stories. In Mark 4:34 it says, *"[Jesus] would not speak to them without using parables."* People love to hear stories. Did you ever notice that when a preacher interrupts his theological message and begins to tell a story, the people suddenly sit up and take notice? This is one of the secrets about keeping an audience involved, and Jesus knew it. We should remember it as well. People listen to and remember stories. I once preached in Edinburgh, Scotland, and told a story about Abraham Lincoln. Some twenty years later, I met a person who had been in the congregation that day, and he was able to repeat the story in almost perfect detail. But he had forgotten everything else I said!

A little aside here, which some people may see as questionable. Preaching is entertainment. Worship is theater. Getting together in the presence of God should be fun! We can experience the joy of the

Lord only in a setting where laughter is permissible, where humor is a medium of communication, and where people are inspired to applaud and cheer and cry. If we are not moved emotionally by what we are seeing and hearing, the message is not truly getting through. It is not our brain which needs to be involved so much as our heart. Without both of them responding to the service, we have missed something essential.

What kind of stories can the preacher tell? All kinds – inspirational stories, personal stories, biblical stories, educational stories, stories which illustrate the new approach we are discussing, stories which capture the interest and imagination of the hearers. Sermons often come from a place of fear, from the need to control, from the traditions of men. Spiritual stories come from love, from hope, from the desire to free people, from the other side of reality.

We can begin with the parables of Jesus. While Paul talks theology, Jesus in his stories talks about the freedom that God has to offer. The Good Samaritan is a perfect example. It says nothing about the fear of God, about being saved, about avoiding hell. Rather, it says that compassion is what discipleship is all about, it says that religion should not divide us, and it reminds us that all people are equal in God's sight. Telling that story and delving into its implications can tell a great deal about the nature of God.

The Prodigal Son is another classic. It doesn't talk about God's judgment but about His acceptance. The parable of the Unforgiving Servant compares God's forgiveness of us with our unwillingness to forgive others. The Pharisee and the Publican is a parable which deals with self-righteousness vs. humility. The gospels are a gold mine of narratives which can be translated into modern terms. This approach captures the imagination of the hearer and can leave a lasting impression.

Another source of powerful stories are devotional magazines like *Guideposts*. Many of these narratives carry a powerful impact and can be the source of memorable lessons about spirituality. At our Christmas Eve services, I would often use a seasonal story from one of these guides in place of a sermon, and the people came to expect it. They would often tell me how much the story meant, subtly letting me know that they preferred stories to my regular sermons!

There are many books available which contain angel stories, tales of remarkable events which can only be explained by angelic intervention. These mystical stories can help people recognize that we are not alone, and can teach them to look for divine intervention in their own lives.

Laypeople should be allowed a larger role in this new approach to worship, and one of the best sources of stories that inspire and uplift can come from their personal experiences. Small groups can give people the courage to tell their stories, which then may be used as featured elements in corporate worship. Hearing a first-hand story like this often has far more impact than one taken from a book. It is a way of training people to look for the activity of God in their daily life.

There's an old joke among clergy: "Ministers are paid to be good; laypeople are good for nothing." It sounds like an insult, but it's a significant truth. A spiritual witness from a lay person carries a different level of truth and conviction than the same thing from a clergyman, from whom such things are expected.

We frequently had members of the congregation share their own experiences during worship, and it never failed to have an emotional impact on the people. I remember one Caucasian woman who was urging support for an organization called The Fresh Air Fund, which brings kids from city ghettos to spend a few weeks in the country during the summer. She had a son who was seven, and they invited an African American boy from Cleveland, named Joe, also seven, to spend two weeks with them. The boys became very close friends, and the woman's son toward the end of that time said urgently to his mother, "Let's not use last names any more. Then maybe people will think that Joe and I are really brothers." That moment was the highlight of the entire service, and people spoke about it for months. She had been more eloquent in three minutes than I was in twenty. Unless there is true emotion in a service, it fails to achieve a level where change can happen. And in my experience, lay witness is a valuable tool in making this happen.

I was chaplain for a quarter century to the Alcoholics

Anonymous group that met in our church. When they had an anniversary banquet and invited other groups to join them, they always featured a guest speaker. These "leads" were among the very best speeches I have ever heard. They were simply their account of their life, their upbringing, their descent into alcoholism, and their rescue by AA. But the stories were told with such self-deprecating humor that the audience laughed and wept and identified with what was being said. These were powerful and memorable stories, and they brought about change in members of the audience. That is the kind of storytelling I would like to see in the new church.

Since the purpose of this approach is to open up the boundaries of what can be used in worship, we should think about including such new elements as dream interpretation. We could begin with the stories of dream interpretation in the Bible – the Joseph saga in the Old Testament, for instance – and then have someone share his or her own dream along with an interpretation, indicating how this has helped them clarify their search for God's direction in their life. If the dream interpretation came from a small group within the church, it would encourage others to join a similar group, as well as helping everyone to take their own dreams more seriously.

The preacher can think about writing his own extended parables, which will force him to think about his message in new terms. This is a much more artistic, and more demanding, form of sermon writing, but it is a technique which will help his message to stay in the hearts and minds of his hearers for a much longer period.

Some years ago, I took a course in story preaching from a preacher/college professor friend of mine. He was a master at this craft, and had a reputation for making his hearers think. He inspired us to be more creative in our preaching, and I discovered immediately that when I used this method, people stopped falling asleep in the pews! They asked more questions as they greeted me at the door, and they shook my hand with a wink, saying, "I knew what you were saying." It was a whole new experience for all of us.

When a preacher delivers a doctrinal sermon, saying in effect that this is the truth and there is no debate about it, the pew sitter has no option but to agree or disagree. But his or her response to a story is quite different. The Bible indicates that Jesus used parables to disguise his meaning.[16] This is not quite accurate. He wanted people to get his meaning, of course, but he wanted them to figure it out for themselves. And so, because they were often confused about his meaning, they had to ponder the outer story until the hidden inner meaning made itself clear. The same thing is true with story sermons. The preacher can choose to explain every symbolic subtlety and do all the thinking for his hearers, or in a narrative sermon he can trust them to think the story through for themselves and decide how it applies to their lives. This process will make the experience much more personal, and therefore easier to remember.

In short, the emphasis needs to change from proclamation and theological instruction to narrative and personal experience. When a congregation makes this switch in its approach, the response will be immediate and dramatic.

Instruction in the Spiritual Laws Instead of Theology[17]

Even though we are trying to get away from theology and focus on spirituality, there still needs to be some sort of instruction during worship, so that the people can grow and add more depth to their faith. A perfect way to do this is by discussing the spiritual laws. There is a great tradition concerning the laws which govern the spirit world; the more we become aware of our spiritual origin, the more these laws impact us. The study of these universal principles can be a major tool for developing significant spiritual understanding in the congregation. What are some of these laws?

The Law of Abundance

When we visualize abundance in our lives, we draw to ourselves the things which we need in order to survive comfortably. There is enough in the universe for everyone. Those resources flow through us in our giving and receiving. "Lack" is the result of giving without receiving. "Hoarding" is the result of receiving without giving. Our goal is to experience abundance, balance, having just enough to fill our needs.

The Law of Action
No matter what our potential gifts or talents, it is only action that brings them to life.

The Law of Allowing
We need to learn the freedom involved in allowing circumstances to be what they are and people to be who they are, whether we agree with them or not.

The Law of Attraction
We attract to ourselves whatever we put the energy of our thoughts into. When we desire something, we can attract it by anticipating its arrival into our life. Jesus referred to this law when he said, *"If you believe, you will receive whatever you ask for in prayer."*[18]

The Law of Accident
When you have low self-esteem, you allow the events of the outside world to control your life. As a result, you always feel like the victim of circumstances you can't control.

The Law of Cause and Effect
Everything happens for a reason. Every action has its own consequences. Every effect has a specific cause. This is similar to Newton's third law of motion: for every action there is an equal and opposite reaction.

The Law of Belief
Whatever you believe can become your reality. Negative beliefs will block positive results.

The Law of Correspondence
What you experience on the outside of your body is a reflection of what is happening inside your body. That is, your outer world reflects your inner world. To make your outside life better, you must change your inner life.

In the place of theology, a pastor could preach many series of sermons on these basic spiritual laws, laws which govern us all, but about which most people know little or nothing. Awareness of how these laws affect us could appreciably change the way in which we experience life.

The Law of Karma

We need to remember that, from the point of view of eternity, our various lifetimes are seen as mere classes in school. They may seem to last forever on this side, but the true perspective from the other side is far different. Each lesson adds to the soul's wisdom, and becomes part of the permanent reservoir of knowledge and truth which is God.

Understanding this karmic principle gives us answers to questions which have always perplexed Christians. Why are some people born rich and others poor, why are some left to starve while others have an abundance of good things? It seems unfair of God, but we know that God cannot be unfair. So there must be another explanation, and karma provides an answer to that apparent inequality. If we can learn that it is in our own best interest to do good, then we will be more highly motivated to live the type of life to which religion has always called us.

Spending time in worship studying the implications of this tremendously important law will do much, not only to instill spiritual principles, but also to encourage members to live a life which will avoid as much negative karma as possible.

Karma is not as eastern a concept as some people would like us to believe. It is actually a Christian principle, and Jesus warned his disciples about its consequences. He said, *"Give to others and God will give to you...The measure you use for others is the one that God will use for you."*[19] *"Do not judge others, so that God will not judge you. For God will judge you in the same way you judge others."*[20] Jesus makes it very clear that we get what we give, that generosity begets generosity, and judgment begets judgment.

So, far from the idea that God is a harsh God, waiting to judge us with cruelty and anger, Jesus is saying that our judgment is in our own hands, that we can determine on Earth how we will be treated in heaven. That is a concept which has been sadly neglected in our day, and which needs to be reinstated as a major consideration of the church. After all, salvation is currently the focus of the church's message – how to avoid hell and be welcomed in heaven. If people took seriously the idea that they are writing the book of their own judgment, a book which will one day be read back to them, it would make a huge difference in how they live.

How does karma work? It is the law of balance, of equilibrium. It is like two people standing in a canoe in the middle of a lake. If one person leans to the left, the boat is going to lean to the left. If he leans too far, the canoe will capsize. The reflex on the part of the other person is to lean to the right, to counteract the first person's action and stabilize the boat. Every action has an equal and opposite reaction.

The canoe is our life. The impulse to lean one way is our tendency to sin. The counter impulse is an effort to atone for the sin. The goal is balance, and we will be judged one day by the amount of balance we have achieved in our lives. But it is we ourselves, not God, who will do the judging. So the whole matter is a very personal affair, and we should want to do the very best job possible with the opportunities which are afforded us.

If we live a life in which we are a cruel husband, we will watch a replay of that life when we return to spirit. Being more objective on the other side than we have been here, we will see the pain we caused, and realize that we earned negative karma during that recent life. In order to regain some balance for ourselves, and to understand how it feels to be a victim, we may elect to become an abused woman in the next life. In this way, the soul can internalize why it is wrong to be abusive.

Abolitionists held the position, before the Civil War, that "If you would not be a slave, you must not be a slaveholder." If we know what it is to be owned and abused by another, we will treat all people with more care. How do we learn how it feels to be that abused person? By living a life in which we are abused. Of course, it works in the opposite way also. A life of love and compassion might gain us additional opportunities to do good, or it might help us to burn off negative karma.

Other Religious Traditions

I have made it quite clear that I am not advocating doing away with Christianity or with Christian practices. They are the backbone of our cultural heritage, and I believe that their absence would do irreparable harm to society. We are not ready to do without this institutional tradition which brings stability and structure to our lives. The only thing I am asking is that the church as a whole – and individual congregations one at a time – confess that their message is metaphorical, that it has value for our spiritual instruction, that it is an essential part of our life and spiritual growth, but that it is not the only true path to God.

In this regard, I think it is imperative that valuable insights from other religious traditions be a regular part of divine worship, so that we can gain from their wisdom and learn how they think about God. We hope that this would reduce the hostility that comes from ignorance of the belief systems of others.

My former congregation had an ongoing relationship for thirty years with a Reform Jewish Temple in town. In later years, this relationship opened up to include other faith traditions, and we called the group The Oneness Fellowship. It included Christians, Jews, Muslims, Hindus, Baha'is, Buddhists, Native Americans, Wiccans and Unitarian Universalists. We came together to explore the spiritual principles of each group and to find common ground on which we could stand together. If we had discussed theology, there would have been chaos in our meetings, but we agreed not to do so. What we discovered was that when we discussed the spiritual principles of the various groups, they sounded surprisingly similar. We were in agreement as long as we talked about the metaphysical aspects of our various faiths. We learned something amazing from that experience, that religious differences do not need to lead to conflict. We truly felt that we had established a special kind of spiritual oneness.

One of the ways in which we can open up channels of

understanding in our new church is to invite those from other traditions to occupy our pulpits to talk about their own spiritual traditions. Or small study groups could focus on various other religious traditions and report to the congregation from time to time on what they have learned. From this, we could gain new insights into the spirit world and reduce cultural tensions in the communities in which we live.

<u>Small Groups</u>

One of the most important new elements that the church should add to its catalog of programs is a small groups ministry. Corporate worship is a large group, a communal experience. So there needs to be an experience at the other end of the spectrum to provide balance, something which includes the kind of intimacy which is impossible in large Sunday morning congregations. Divine worship on the Lord's Day is supposed to be a celebration of what God has done in the lives of the people during the previous week. The problem is that most people have nothing to celebrate because they have not given themselves an opportunity to focus on the activity of God in their lives. As a result, worship becomes a kind of empty routine.

Small group ministries can change that situation. When we used them in our church, they worked a revolution. The worldwide Christian population started out as a small group, and ended up changing the world. Local ministries of this sort could very well end up changing the church. The majesty of morning worship and the intimacy of a small group are complementary experiences which can reinforce each other and allow the worshipper to have the fullest kind of spiritual experience.

Our small groups were limited to six or seven people. The members contracted to meet weekly or bi-weekly for a year and then disband. Each person agreed to attend all the meetings because when one was missing the dynamics changed noticeably. We used prepared materials, and there are many to choose from, but it is also possible to write your own. The aim is to get to know the others in the group as thoroughly as possible. This is achieved through a series of exercises in which members respond to questions or situations which reveal how they think and feel. Once intimacy is established, remarkable things begin to happen. People discover that when they reveal their inner self, far from being judged and rejected, they are embraced and cherished, and this realization creates a kind of joy that many of them have never known. And this in turn can lead to an entirely new level of connection with God.

One side effect of this sharing of lives is the freedom to reveal mystical spiritual experiences, many of which have never been told before. There is a sort of awe that creeps over the group as they realize the variety of ways in which God can touch their lives. And it frees the members to be more open to those mysteries in their own lives, to look for them, to celebrate them, and to share them with others outside the group in a kind of personal ministry. These groups can prepare their members to speak in the morning worship services, as we noted above. The group gives them the courage to tell their story in public, and their witness to God's activity in their lives has a ripple effect throughout the congregation.

Small groups can have specially designed experiences which would never be possible on a Sunday morning. For instance, a trust walk is a special way of learning what it means to be guided by the Holy Spirit. And an exercise called Jesus' Hands teaches a powerful message about our connectedness to Christ and through him to our neighbor. [See appendix]

In small groups, we are free to do guided meditations which can help members learn to communicate one-on-one with God. I remember the first time I was part of a group doing a guided meditation. The leader had us set up a place in our minds where we could meet with Jesus and have a personal conversation. He suggested a ring of stones outdoors somewhere, near a lake, with a fire in the center, and had us work on this image before we were ready to invite Jesus in. I went deep into the experience, but was shocked to find that my conversation ring was overgrown with weeds and cluttered with trash. It was so messy and uncared for that I couldn't imagine meeting Jesus there. It became clear to me that there were messes in my life that I had to clean up before I could deepen my relationship with God. That, for me, was a powerful metaphor; it provided an embarrassing truth about myself that I would not have seen without the meditation. It inspired me to make some changes, and those changes made my later meditative life much more satisfying.

Personal Devotions
 There is a third aspect to the fully functional spiritual life, after divine worship and small group membership. And that is personal devotions. Taking time each day for prayer, Bible reading and meditation helps to make more personal the truths learned in the other experiences. A person's small group can give "homework" to its members – a book to read which will be discussed at the next meeting, a biblical passage to be studied with notations to be shared with the group. The group can develop prayer lists which members can use as guides in their own private prayer time. Or they can participate in so-called "prayer assaults" during which all the members pray for the same thing at the same time every day for a month. A new understanding of prayer as directed energy will help members see why this sort of thing works. The group would keep a record of the goals of each assault and the results which were observed. Such an effort will convince everyone of the efficacy of prayer when it is undertaken seriously, as opposed to how lightly prayer is often treated by church groups at present.
 We have said that since we are all part of God, we are all connected. This makes it clear that when we help someone else, we are really helping ourselves. The Golden Rule has always contained this wisdom in its simple formula – *"Do for others what you want them to do for you."*[21] At the very deepest soul level, that other person *is* you. Seen in this light, you can be aware that karma is deeply imbedded in the Christian belief system. When we all learn to be our brother's keeper, the Kingdom will have come.

****

 The challenge before us is to change the church's focus away from theology, from insisting that its story is literal history and its plan of salvation is the only route to God. The church leadership must understand the uses and the valuable potential of myth, and realize that the truth of the Kingdom is never final or fully understood. Therefore, it needs to gain the humility and the maturity to admit that the church's story is a work in progress. The church must also become more open to the input of the Holy Spirit than it is at present. If it can do this, if it can see these modern revelations as gifts from God which will expand its current myth and make it more exciting and attractive, it will be ready to minister to the newer generations which are coming into the world. These people already have an updated version of spiritual software installed. They know that we are spiritual beings who have immediate access to the spirit world. They know that we do not need to be "saved." But we do need to be reminded of the high purpose for which we have chosen to incarnate. The church must appeal to these new generations, or it will die.

God will continue to reveal His truth forever. Let us hope that the church will be up to the challenge of mediating this new truth, rather than being chained to its old message forever. The church needs God far more than God needs the church. Let us work together to turn the Christian myth into a story so compelling that coming generations will fall in love with it, and work together to move humanity one step closer to establishing the Kingdom of God on Earth.

Appendix

Trust Walk

In this event, members are divided into pairs, and one of them is blindfolded. The other person then proceeds to give the dependent person the richest possible experience, without any verbal communication – touching things, climbing stairs, creating sounds, stimulating all the senses except sight.

Done well, this can create in the person being led an extraordinary sense of being cared for, of trust for the partner. And this increases the sense of God's guidance and care in his/her own life.

Following the exercise, the couples discuss their feelings, both about leading and being led. That experience can produce some memorable insights.

Jesus' Hands

This exercise involves the whole group. The people stand in a circle while the leader remains outside. The members all close their eyes and join hands. The leader speaks to them about the hand in their right hand, saying that it is the hand of their neighbor. He encourages them to examine the hand with their fingers, and try to imagine who the person is from the feel of their hand. He talks about the need that that neighbor has for his love and care.

Then he tells the group to feel the hand in their left hand, and to realize that it is the hand of Jesus. He tells them to communicate with Jesus through touching his hand. Then he makes the point that each person is the connection between Jesus and his neighbor.

The people then drop their hands and take a step backward. The leader talks about loneliness and speaks of the many people who never feel the touch of another hand. Finally, he has them take a step forward toward the center of the circle and reach out for the others' hands, still with their eyes closed.

The members need to be encouraged to keep their eyes closed, in spite of a temporary inability to find the hands of the others. At first, this produces a sense of lostness and disconnection which can be quite dramatic, and when the connection is remade, the relief is amazing. The leader may want to help some who are seriously lost. There is a lot to discuss after such an exercise.

There are dozens of such experiences a small group can share, including healing and prayer circles, each one creating a new sense of closeness with each other, and a deepening awareness of God in their midst.

Story Credits

*A Fear of Horses – Loretta Miller
An Angel Voice - Sherrie Thomas-Woodside
     Duffsherrie@yahoo.com
*A Child's Frightening Memory - Annie Lethcoe
A Phobia Cured – Sherri Silesky
     nfpain.blogspot.com
A Pre-Birth Premonition – Sandi Johnson
     redhotdots@yahoo.com
A Shared Dream – Colin A. Campbell
A Visit from Denise – Marshan Raub
*An Angel of Light – Sage
Coming Back as a Baby – Colleen
My Grandson's Former Life – Susan Vann
     Wasilla, Alaska
He Was a Little Girl – Parkin
Killed By the Nazis? – Meg McLeod
     honeybear705@yahoo.com
Memories Before I Was Born – Daniel Waterman
Something Special for Me – Norma Jean Netzley
     Submitted by her daughter:
     Jeanne Ellen (Netzley) Nelson
     Jeannels444@aol.com
The Memory of a Fire - Sylvia Caballero
The "Moving" Picture - Christine Sherborne
     chris@colourstory.com
     www.colourstory.com
*Traveling Outside the Car – Lena Bettis

*Email address changed; author cannot be contacted.
All of the authors listed above gave permission for their stories to be published on our website: www.beyondreligion.com. We attempted to contact all of them for this book, but some did not respond. If there are any changes needed, they will be made in subsequent editions.

Notes

[1] Matt. 16:19

[2] Luke 23:43

[3] Matt. 6:14-15

[4] Marco Iacoboni is Professor of Psychiatry and Biobehavioral Sciences and Director of the Transcranial Magnetic Stimulation Lab at the Ahmanson-Lovelace Brain Mapping Center.

[5] John 14:12

[6] Evolution is a totally different issue than reincarnation. We may have evolved from other forms, but we do not revert to those forms in reincarnation. The issue is controlled by soul development.

[7] Matt 16:19

[8] There are 73 books in the Roman Catholic Bible.

[9] Bible Myths and Their Parallels in Other Religions, 1882, p. 198.

[10] With thanks to: http://www.youtube.com/watch?v=sD9f0XU_S78

[11] See Numbers 22:22ff

[12] www.beyondreligion.com

[13] Matt. 16:14

[14] John 9:2

[15] They *are* available, however, to our subconscious, which is what makes past-life therapy possible.

[16] Mark 4:12

[17] With thanks to the following sites:
http://www.greatdreams.com/vision1.htm
http://www.infuzemag.com/The-Spiritual-Laws-Associated-with-Metaphysics.php

[18] Matt. 21:22

[19] Luke 6:38

[20] Matt. 7:1-2

[21] Matt. 7:12

www.ingramcontent.com/pod-product-compliance
Lightning Source LLC
LaVergne TN
LVHW051641080426
835511LV00016B/2431